Psalms in a Poem

THOMAS D. "DENNY" HAHN

PUBLISHED BY
OUR WRITTEN LIVES, LLC

Copyright ©2021 Thomas Denzil "Denny" Hahn

Library of Congress Cataloging-in-Publication Data
Hahn, Thomas D. "Denny"
Psalms in a Poem

Library of Congress Control Number: 2021914613

ISBN: 978-1-942923-49-7 (paperback)
978-1-942923-50-3 (hardback)

Dedication

This book is dedicated to the five most influential men in my life, next to Jesus Christ:

#1. My father, Gary Lee Hahn, who has prayed for me every day of my life since he knew he was going to be a father. He was my first piano teacher; I was age four.

#2. My uncle, Rev. Thomas Lynn "Uncle Tommy" Craft, who has been with me since the beginning and was my mentor and teacher at Jackson College of Ministries.

#3. My childhood pastor, Rev. Louis J. McDaniel, a converted street-brawler and one of the most gentle giants I've ever known.

#4. Rev. Charles Grisham, in whose home I lived and under whose ministry I sat in awe, as he patiently taught me the ins and outs of the work of the Lord.

#5. Rev. James "Papa K" Kilgore, whose love for souls extended around the world and blazed a trail for countless others to follow.

These five men came before me and influenced everything meaningful in my life. I owe each of them a debt of gratitude I can never repay. I often share from their stores of wit and wisdom, which they so willingly gave to me and everyone around them.

Acknowledgments

I thank the many people who have helped and encouraged me in the writing of Psalms in a Poem. First and foremost, would be Jesus Christ, who inspired and led me to the creation of this poetic work.

Next, would be my late wife Deborah Barraza "Debbie" Hahn, who was my #1 cheerleader and who was always ready to hear the next chapter all the way from the beginning to the end of Psalms in a Poem. She listened intently to all one hundred and fifty poems.

Then there was Pam Nolde, who reviewed the book and said it was "a prayer journey."

Also, Bishop Anthony Mangun, Sr. Pastor of Pentecostals of Alexandria (POA), who encouraged me to promote the book.

My sister, Judy Schuldt, helped me with typing and proofing, as did my nephews Bradley and Tanner Schuldt, my daughters Courtney Smith and Ashley Wiechman, and my cousin Annalisa Anderson.

My parents, Gary and Mary Hahn, bore with patience the painstaking process by which I obtained and read through the chapters of the book while recovering from an auto accident which impaired my speech for several months.

Of particular note is the special encouragement of Bishop Thomas L. Craft of First Pentecostal Church, Jackson, Mississippi, who encouraged me in the formative stages of the book.

Also, Pastor Mark Jobe of Gateway Church was an enthusiastic encourager of the book.

Finally, I give acknowledgment to my publisher, Rachael K. Hartman of Our Written Lives, LLC, without whose expertise this book would not have come to fruition.

And a special acknowledgment to everyone who reads Psalms in a Poem. May this book bless you to read it as much as it has blessed me to write it.

Foreword

No three words can describe Denny Hahn. To understand his book, you need to know a little about Denny.

He is brilliant, one of the smartest men I know. He's the best musician I have been acquainted with. He was good at math and reading at the age of four. He's excellent in music, and can duplicate classic pieces without notes.

But even with all of his talent, if he had a flat tire on the right front, he might change the left rear. Menial things mean nothing to Denny. He thinks in a different realm.

There are few geniuses in the world that are true Christians. Denny is one of them. He has a pure heart, and his motives are the same.

After he wrote the first few chapters, I encouraged him to finish this book because it would be the first one of it's kind that I know of.

You will enjoy reading it just like the KJV Bible itself. It has rhythm, flow, and meaning, which are the characteristics of Hebrew scholarship.

I recommend Denny and this book. It's a poem of the entire Psalms. Only Denny would attempt this project.

I love him very much, and believe in him, and pray for his success in this world and the world to come.

Bishop Thomas L. Craft
FIRST PENTECOSTAL CHURCH
JACKSON, MISSISSIPPI

Introduction

You may be wondering why someone would feel the need to rewrite a perfectly good book such as the Psalms. Psalms is already an inspiring book, poetic in nature and description.

Well, the idea came to me as a challenge. What if Psalms could be put into rhyme without sacrificing the core truths and inspirations?

I thought this idea was from the Lord, so I acted on it.

Thirty-one chapters into my writing, I had a serious car accident which left me speech-challenged for several months.

Forty-five days after my accident, I cried out to the Lord for help. How could I continue my writing task when I couldn't even carry on a conversation?

The answer came. "Don't worry, son, just go on to sleep, and I will wake you when it's time."

Three and a half hours after I went to bed that night, the Lord awakened me. "It's time!"

So every night I went to the front room where He would give me rhymes, a little at a time until it was finally done.

Words and phrases like pennies from Heaven would fall into my mind's eye, and I would write. Once I started, the poetry flowed out from the depths of my soul, through pen-strokes back to God who gave the inspiration to me.

I couldn't even talk, but God was giving me beautiful poetic verses! To Him be all the glory!

CHAPTER 1
"Blessed is the Man"

Blessed is the man, / Who, when he walks, / Walks not in the counsel / Of evil men // Blessed is the man, / Who, when he stands, / Stands far away from where / Sin can get him //
Blessed is the man, / Who, when he sits, / Sits far from scorners who / Could do him in // But the Lord's Law is His / Supreme delight / He thinks about God's law / Both day and night //
He is like a tree / With good roots and good water / His life will bear fruit / That will last and will prosper //
The ungodly ones are soon / Driven away / They won't stand in judgment / Or rule with the saints //
The Lord knows the way of / His children, His own / But the name of the ungodly / Soon shall be gone

CHAPTER 2
"I Have Set My King"

Why do all the heathen rage? / And their followers, thus feeble, / Kings and rulers come as one, / Fighting God and all His people //
Thinking they can break away / From His appointed judgment day / The Lord laughs upon His throne / In His wrath they cry and moan //
I have set my King on High / Once begotten, twice alive / All the nations will be Thine / For the uttermost is Mine // With your scepter made of iron / You shall break them all like clay / Listen to the God of Zion / Serve the Lord with fear today //
And rejoice with trembling, too / Seek His favor, don't delay // Live so He will smile on you // Trust Him, He will see you through

CHAPTER 3
"My Protecting Shield"

They increase who want me dead / Some would love to take my head / Many say my soul is lost / Forsaken --- think about it! //

You are my protecting Shield / Lord, You keep my head held high / (My soul gloried in the Lord, / And He heard me when I cried) //
I lay down in peaceful rest / And awakened, surely blessed / Many round me have arrayed // Arise, Oh Lord, and save the day //
You have struck them on the cheek / You have broken all their teeth / You save whosoever will / And You bless Your people still //
Think about it!

CHAPTER 4
"Stand in Awe"

God, You are my Righteousness / Hear me when I call / You save me from my distress / Please don't let me fall //
People, please don't turn to shame / Don't be violent, don't be vain / Think how God preserves the man / Who calls on the great I AM //
Stand in awe, please do not sin / Be still, set your heart on Him / Think about His Righteousness / Trust in Him, and He will bless //
He will shine His light on us / Gladden our hearts with increase / I will lay me down, and sleep / For the Lord gives sweet relief

CHAPTER 5
"Be My Leader, Oh My Lord"

Listen to my words, my Lord / Please hear all my meditation / Hearken to my cry, my King / God of all my consolation //
Early will I lift my voice / I will look to You on High / I will not bless wicked choice / Evil men cannot come nigh //
Foolishness shall fall by You / Those who work iniquity / Vile, deceitful people, too / But God's people have mercy //
I will reverence Your house / Lead me, Lord, in Righteousness / Make my paths plain to my eyes / Keep me from all faithlessness //
Some hold wickedness inside / They speak flatteries and lies / They are wise in their own eyes / Cast out those proud rebels //
Let Your people trust in You / Rejoice and shout for Your Defense / All who love Your Name will have / Righteousness and Recompense //
You will bless with Shield and Sword / Be my Leader, Oh my Lord / You will bless with Shield and Sword / Be my Leader, Oh my Lord

CHAPTER 6
"My Tears Are My Offering"

Oh Lord, please take me higher / Leave the chast'ning rod behind / Please have mercy on me / I am weak, but Thou art strong //
I know You can heal me / Even if my bones do grind / My soul is also grinding / How long, Oh Lord, how long? //
Oh Lord, deliver my soul / Make me a prize of mercy / In death, I cannot praise You / The dead give Thee no thanks //
I cry so much my bed swims / My tears are my offering / My eyes are worn with crying / Because of my enemies //
Depart from me, iniquity / The Lord has heard my moaning / In all my supplication / He will receive my prayer //
To all who are my enemies / You will have vexing sorrow / And if you come back for me / Your shame will meet you there

CHAPTER 7
"Let Wickedness Be No More"

Oh Lord my God, in You I trust / I know You save from all persecution / You make a way, lest my soul stray / Lest the enemy tear me like a lion //
Oh Lord my God, if I have sinned / If I hold iniquity in my hands / If I render evil for good / (But I have delivered all that I could) //
I deserve persecution / And that my name be remembered no more / I think how You arise, Lord / And bring judgment on my enemies //
Your people worship You, Lord / In righteousness and integrity
Let wickedness be no more / Establish the just, for You are Righteous //
Try the hearts and try the reins / God is the defender of the upright / God will test the righteous ones / He wars daily against all wickedness //
For those who turn not from wrongs / He bends His bow of injuriousness / Death to the persecutors / Sinners who make mischief and bring forth lies //

The pit reserved for others / Into that same ditch, they fall and then they die / The mischief of the wicked shall return on his own head / His violence shall fall upon himself as he falls dead //

The Lord rules in Righteousness / I sing praise to the Name of the Most High / The Lord is always Righteous / I sing praise to the Name of the Most High

CHAPTER 8

"Lord, You Are Our Lord"

Lord, You are our Lord / Your Name is Most Excellent in all the earth / You ride on the stars / From when we were babies You gave us our worth //

Your enemies rise / You slay all the avenging enemy's power //

I look at the skies / Sun, moon, stars, all change from this hour to that hour //

And You made it so / Why should You care so for a poor, sinful man? / Yet You visit him / You made him just below angels in Your Plan //

Gave honor to him / He glories and reigns over all of the earth / Placed under his feet / Sheep, oxen, beasts, birds and fish in this world dwell //

Lord, You are our Lord / Your Name is Most Excellent in all the earth / Lord, You are our Lord / Your Excellent Name they endeavor to tell

CHAPTER 9

"God is a Refuge"

I will praise You, Lord, with all of my heart / I will declare all / Your Wonderful Works / I will be thankful and joyful in You / Enemies fall at Your Presence and Worth //

You have protected my rights from Your throne / Rebuking the heathen, destroying the bad / My enemy, you shall come to your end / Your lands and heritage have all been had //

But the Lord liveth forever and ever / A place of judgment is the Lord's throne / Righteous from unrighteousness He will sever / At His Judgment Bar is the Lord's Throne / God is a refuge for all the oppressed / He knows just how to deliver from trouble / All who know Your Name will be truly blessed / They trust You, call You, You come on the double! //

Sing praises to the Lord who lives in Zion / Tell all the people His Marvelous Works / He protects His blood-washed ones, Judah's Lion / The humble heart's cry He will hear, and not shirk //

Have mercy on me, Oh Lord, hear my plea / I suffer trouble from them that hate me / You lift me out of the bondage of death / I will praise You as long as I have breath //

You are my Savior, my God, and my King / The heathen are sunk down, they've lost everything // They set a trap for the righteous to fall in / In the same trap which they laid, they are taken //

The Lord is well-known by the Judgment He gives / The wicked is snared for as long as he lives / I meditate upon Your Wondrous Works, Oh Lord / And I pause to think about Your Shield and Your Sword //

All wicked souls and all nations who forget God / Shall be turned to Hell, but the needy shall not fall / The poor and needy shall see the things God hath wrought / Rise up, Oh Lord, judge the heathen, be Lord of all

CHAPTER 10
"The Lord is the King"

Why do You hide from me, Oh my Lord? / Why do You stand far away when I seek You? / Wicked men enrich themselves for the poor / Let them fall in the things that they have turned to //

Wicked men brag as they feast and they gorge / They bless themselves, but they abhor the Lord / The countenance of a wicked man's pride / Will not allow God to walk at His side //

The ways of the wicked are grievous to God / He has no fear of the chastening rod / And as for his enemies, he laughs at them / He thinks that adversity is far from him //

He curses and lies and deceives all his neighbors / His mischief and pride consume all of his labors / He lurks for the innocent soul to accost / Lays wait for the poor without thought for the cost //

He secretly waits in his devious den / He murders the poor—they mean nothing to him / He thinks God is blind and afraid of the dark / Please rise up, Oh Lord, and please don't miss Your mark //

The wicked condemns God and thinks He is free / His judgment is coming, he just doesn't see / The poor and the fatherless God will deliver / The wicked arm break until there's not a sliver //

The Lord is the King and the heathen are perished / The humble are glad and their hearts are encouraged / God will heal the fatherless and oppressed / Until all the earth will be happy at rest

CHAPTER 11
"His Holy Throne"

All my trust is in the Lord / I will not flee like a bird / When the wicked bend their bow / And take aim with their arrow //

They shoot at the upright heart / Try to kill him in the dark / If they kill foundation truths / What good can the righteous do? //

God sits on His Holy Throne / And from there He reigns alone / He looks down with loving eyes / Righteous souls the Lord does try //

But the wicked, violent soul / Shall see snares, fire and brimstone / And a tempest in their cup / But the righteous He lifts up

CHAPTER 12
"The Finest Things"

We need some help right now, Lord / Godliness is in short supply / Faithful folks are failing fast / Many speak to please themselves / Flatteries and lies prevail / God shall cut them off at last //

Lying lips, deceitful tongues / Stubborn ones who force their way through / Thinking, what can the Lord do? //

Poor and needy hearts He knows / He will rise to fight for those / All oppressors will be through //

God's words are the finest things / Purifying priests and kings / As silver, seven times tried //

The poor and the needy souls / Preserved now and forever / You shall keep them in Your care //

But the wicked walk astray / When dark souls do lead the way / There remains no comfort there

CHAPTER 13
"Hear Me Now"

When will You remember me? / Lord, am I forgotten? / Even though Your Face I seek / Still it is quite hidden // I need Your Light in my soul / As I sorrow daily / Shall my enemy control / All pertaining to me? //
Please consider, hear me now / Oh, my Lord Most Holy / Give clear vision to mine eyes / Sleep of death far from me //
I will not give place today / To my enemy's words / Lest he say, I have prevailed / And rejoice against the Lord //
But I put my trust in You / Mercy shall sustain me / Your Salvation sees me through / I will sing before Thee

CHAPTER 14
"God Never Fails"

The fool does not believe in God / He works corrupt abomination / Not one of them does any good / The Lord looks down with consternation //
From good works they have turned aside / Their filthiness they cannot hide / Not one has goodness down inside / They eat My People up alive //
But there is Knowledge of the Lord / When Fear and Righteousness are merged / The wicked bow before the poor / When in God's Refuge sin is purged //
And when the Lord's Amazing Grace / Brings back His Jacob to one place / The sound of laughter will prevail / Because the Lord God never fails

CHAPTER 15
"He Who Walks with Uprightness"

What kind of person shall abide / In Your Tabernacle? / And who shall live within / Your Holy Hill? // He who walks with uprightness /

Doing righteous deeds, and / Speaking truth with pure heart / Speaks no ill //

He with no backbiting tongue / Who treats his neighbor well / Who will not speak against his friend / The wicked people are condemned //

He honors those who fear the Lord / He makes a promise, keeps his word / Takes no advantage from His neighbor / Will not give up the innocent //

And he that does these things shall stand / And never be moved from the land / He who walks with uprightness / Shall never be moved from the land

CHAPTER 16
"You Are My Portion"

Oh God, You are One / Who is keeping me alive / I put my trust in You / And my soul, it will survive // Oh God, You are my Lord

There is no one like You / As for Your Saints on Earth / Their Excellence is true //

My soul delights in these / But sorrows shall remain / To those who give to false gods / I shall not call their names //

For Lord, You are my Portion, / Inheritance and Cup / My heritage is goodly / For this I lift You up //

You give me righteous counsel / For You have tried my reins / The darkness is as noonday / The mountain as a flame //

I call upon You always / You are at my right hand / I know I shall not be moved / For You gave me this land //

My heart within is gladdened / And I rejoice in You / And I shall be most hopeful / For You shall bring me through //

I will not see corruption / Within Your Path of Life / Your Presence is Joy's Fullness / And Pleasure without strife

CHAPTER 17

"I Will Surely Follow You"

Hear the righteous cause, Oh Lord / Listen to my cry / Give ear to my prayer, Oh Lord / My lips do not lie //
Let my guidance come from You / With equality / You are able, Oh my Lord / To guide what I speak //
You have proved my heart, Oh God / Seen me in the night / I have chosen to walk clean / And to speak upright //
Other men have strayed from You / They have been destroyed / I will surely follow You / And their paths avoid //
I know You will hear me, Lord / Hear me when I pray / Show Your lovingkindness, Lord / Trustworthy always //
You save by Your Power, Lord / From all enemies / Watch the Apple of Your Eye / Hide me in Your Wings //
Many enemies oppress / They are all around / Full of their deceit and lies / Arrogant and proud //
They surround us by the way / Eyes down to the earth / Like a lion hunting prey / Where young lions lurk //
Rise up, Lord, and throw him down / From his wicked perch / He whose treasuries are found / Full of empty worth //
His tradecraft is wickedness / Wicked children, too / I will seek Your righteousness / And to walk with You

CHAPTER 18

"The Source of My Strength"

Forever I will love You, Lord / You are the Source of my strength / You are the Rock on which I stand / You are the Fortress in my land //
You are the Deliverer at my hand / You are the God whom I serve / You are the Strength of my reserve / You are the Trust that gives me nerve //
You are the Shield of my defense / You are the Strength of my preservation / You are my Hiding Place in the Holy Hill //
I will call upon You, Lord / You are worthy to be praised / Even when death's sorrows come / Even when I am afraid //

When all Hell tries to oppress / I call You in my distress / I cried to the Lord my God / And the Lord God heard my voice //

From His Temple my God heard / He heard my cry, my every word / Then God thundered with His Voice / The earth shook, the mountains trembled //

When He breathed smoke from His Nostrils / Fire from His Mouth, coals were kindled / The heavens bowed and gave him homage / He walked upon the thick darkness / Upon the cherub's wings He flew / And made the night His rendezvous / Thick clouds, dark waters were all His / Brilliant hailstones, fiery mist / And all the heavens heard His Roar / When the LORD GOD / rained hail and fire / The arrows of the Lord are many / Lightnings and disconsolations //

Rivers floods, oceans and seas / The foundations of all the nations / All were seen at Your command / You drew me from many waters //

From my enemy's strong hands / You saved all my sons and daughters / Brought me to a better place / Delighted just to give me grace //

I have walked in righteousness / With clean hands that You could bless / I have kept Your Godly Ways / From Your Ways I have not strayed //

You gave judgments that were true / And Your rules I kept in view / I walked upright with my God / Daily far from sin I trod //

God has given what is right / He saw clean hands in His Sight / Mercy is to mercy shown / And the upright will be known //

Purity shall purify / The wicked run, but they can't hide / The afflicted You will save / But the haughty have no shade //

You light my way in the night / Turn my darkness into light / Through You I have won in battle / Scaled a wall without a ladder //

And Your way is perfect still / All Your Word is tried and true / You protect those in Your Will / A Shield to all who trust in You //

Who is God besides the Lord? / Who is a Rock like our God? / God gives strength and perfect graces / And sets me upon high places //

He gives me the strength to war / Arms to break a bow of steel / His Word is my Shield and Sword / His Meekness makes me genteel //

Through Him my feet did not slip / And my enemies knew my grip / From my wounds they could not rise / Under my feet they did lie //

You have made me battle-strong / Conquered my foes all along / Their necks were before my sword / They cried out unto the Lord //

But He would not answer them / They blew like dust in the wind / Swept like dirt within the street / And You helped me keep the peace //

As the heathen to me flee / Unknown nations shall serve me / They will hear me, and obey / They will serve me, and not stray / As the others fade away / And in hiding are afraid / You are my Lord and my Rock / My saving God, whom I exalt //

You avenge those who would harm / Subdue my people from alarm / You deliver from all harm / You lift me up from all alarm //

You keep me from the violent man / I give thanks to the Great I AM / Among the unsaved I will sing / Praises to Your Name, Oh my King //

You give great deliverance / Tender mercies that are sure / To Your anointed / Unto David and his seed forevermore

CHAPTER 19
"Upright Confession"

All the heavens tell Your Glory / And the skies show off Your Work / Day by day they tell the story / Night by night they never shirk //

There is no form of speech or language / Without which their voice is heard / The skyline moves throughout the earth / The constellation's testament //

Just like a bridegroom's covenant / Or as a strong man runs a race / God's Power from His Heavenly Place / Moves through the circle of the earth //

With fervent heat and blinding light / God's law is perfect, changing men / God's testimony makes men wise / God's statutes make the heart rejoice //

Because His rules are always right //

A Godly fear will keep one clean / Through God's Power forever / God's Judgments every one are true / And righteous altogether //

They have more worth than all the gold / A lifetime could acquire / More sweetness than the honeycomb / And honey much desired //

Your Ways do keep Your servant warned / And keeping them brings great reward / As God reveals our secret sins //

Lord, please cleanse me from within /

Keep me from wrong assumptions, Lord / And prideful sin, the great transgression / Let not these things come over me / And I shall give upright confession //

With words and meditation right / My strong Redeemer, in Your sight / Let my words and thoughts be upright / My strong Redeemer, in Your sight

CHAPTER 20
"The Lord Hears"

May the Lord hear you when you cry / And His name defend you / And send you help from the High One / Strength for you from out of Zion //

May God receive your offerings / Your tithings and your ministries / Now take a pause to meditate / On all His Wondrous Works //

May God give you the right heartbeat / And show you how you ought to think / In Your Salvation we rejoice / And in Your Name we make our choice //

Thus may God grant all your petitions / The Lord keeps His anointed ones / He hears them from His Holy Throne / He saves them with His Powerful Hand //

Some put their trust in chariots / Some put their trust in fast horses / We trust in the Name of the Lord / Their trust is broken when they fall //

But we stand upright through it all / Because the Lord hears when we call / Yes, we stand upright through it all / Because the Lord hears when we call

CHAPTER 21
"Exalt Yourself"

Your Strength, Oh Lord / Brings the king joy / Your Salvation, Oh God / Causes him to rejoice //

You gave the king / His heart's desire / And You answered his prayer / When to You he inquired //

You come before / The king and bless / Through Your Goodness, Oh Lord / A gold crown tops his head //

He asked for life / You set him free / For You gave him new life / For all eternity //

He glories in / Salvation, Lord / Your Honor and Glory / To him You afford // His blessing lasts / Eternally / And Your Countenance, Lord / Makes him happy and free / The King's heart trusts

In You, dear Lord / And Your Goodness and Mercy / Keep his heart restored //

Your hand will fight / Your enemies / And Your Power shall reach / To all those who hate Thee //

You throw them in / Your oven, Lord / You will swallow them up / Soon they shall be no more //

Their work shall be / Abandoned, Lord / And their children forgotten / Who knew not the Lord //

For they all thought / To stop Your Song / They imagined bad things / But they turned out all wrong //

And when they think / They've turned away / Then Your Arrows will sing / From the strings to their face //

Exalt Yourself / Lord, You are strong / We will sing and will praise / You for all the day long

CHAPTER 22
"Save Me from the Lion's Roar"

My God, why did You leave me / Without help when to You I screamed? / Even though to You I cried / In agony both day and night //

But Most Holy are You, raise / We songs to You of perfect praise / Abraham trusted in You / And Isaac and Jacob did, too //

They cried and You delivered / When they trusted You, You came through / But I am in the low spot / People see me as a dark blot //

And look on me with such scorn / Wonder why I was ever born / They laugh and shoot out the lip / Shake their heads, wave their fingertip //

They say, "He trusted the Lord / That the Lord would deliver him / Let God deliver him now / He sure delighted in Him" //

But You took me from the womb / You called me as a baby / Amniotic sac's sweet tomb / From in my mother's belly //

Be not far from me, my God / Trouble is quite near me / Strong bulls have beset me 'round / And stared at me with open mouths //
Poured out am I like water / Disjointed, waxy heart, loose bowels / Like a broken vase am I / Tongue sticks to the roof of my mouth //
At death's door, dogs circle by / My hands and feet pierced as I cry / My bones are all out of joint / Men stare as if I disappoint //
They split my clothes among them / And gambled for my priestly robe / Do not be far from me, Lord / Please come deliver my soul //
Save me from the lion's roar / From all enemy's power / I will shout Your Name, dear Lord / Praise You from the temple door //
If you fear God, praise Him / Jacob's seed, glorify Him / Israel, do fear the Lord / Affliction He won't abhor //
When you call, He will not hide / Your cry goes up to the Lord / I praise God with His Children / Pay my vows unto the Lord //
Humble souls shall have plenty / Seekers shall all praise the Lord / Heart for our God is eternal / All the earth shall turn to God //
All of the people shall worship / For the Kingdom is the Lord's / He is the Ruler of nations / The blessed ones eat and worship //
The dying saints do all praise Him / None can keep himself alive / God will always have a People / Numbered by Him for His time

CHAPTER 23

"The Lord is My Shepherd"

Because the Lord is my Shepherd / I shall not want or lack for any need / And He leads me to green pastures / Beside still waters daily I shall feed //
My soul He is restoring / He leads me on a righteous journey / Though I walk through death's valley / I shall not be afraid, for You are there //
Your Rod and Staff are comfort to me / And when my enemies haunt me / You give anointing as only You can / You spread a table smartly //
I overflow, empowered by Your Touch / Goodness and Mercy follow / And I shall dwell forever in Your House / Yes, I shall dwell forever in Your House

CHAPTER 24
"That Glorious King"

The planet Earth belongs to God / He rules and reigns entirely / Land and sea, animals, plants / And all of humanity //

Out of the seas, He birthed the lands / Mounts, hills, plains and valleys / Who will go up the Hill of the Lord? / Who may remain in His Holy of Holies? //

Only the clean of hands and pure of heart / Free of vain pride and deceitful vanity / He shall obtain blessing from the Most High / Righteous Salvation as to God he draws nigh //

We are the generation who seeks Him / We seek Your Holy Face, Oh God of Jacob / Meditate on Your Grace, Oh God of Jacob / Lift up your heads, Oh ye gates of deliverance //

And be lifted up, doors of eternal praise / As the Glorious King of all ages steps in / Who can be so majestic and full of all glory? / The Lord is the Glorious King, strong and mighty //

The Lord is the Glorious King, strong in battle / Lift up your heads, Oh ye gates of deliverance / And be lifted up, doors of eternal praise / As the Glorious King of all ages steps in //

Who can be so majestic and full of all glory? / The Lord is this Glorious King, strong and mighty / The Lord is this Glorious King, strong in battle / Only He is the One who can be that Glorious King //

Lift up your heads, Oh ye gates of deliverance / And be lifted up, doors of eternal praise / As the Glorious King of all Ages steps in / Only He is the One who can be that Glorious King //

Who can be so majestic and full of all glory? / Lord of land, sea and sky / And all things that lie beneath / Only He is the One who can be that Glorious King //

CHAPTER 25
"Keeper of My Soul"

I look to You and You alone, Lord / You are the Keeper of my soul / I lean entirely upon You, God / Don't let my enemies take control //

Please keep all souls who wait on You, Lord / From the transgressors' violent ways / Show me Your ways, teach me Your paths, Lord / Let Your Truth guide the road that I take //

You are the God of my salvation / It is Your Face I seek night and day / Show me Your tender Mercy and Favor / Since time began, Your Love has brought them //

Blot out my sins, my many transgressions / Goodness and Mercy, follow me in / The Lord is Good, the Lord is Righteous / He will teach sinners His Holy Ways //

Mercy and Truth complete His Covenant, / His Testimonies are full of grace: / Mercy and Truth complete His Covenant, / His Testimonies are full of grace //

For Your Name's sake pardon my sin, Lord / I cannot bear sin's burden alone / Who fears the Lord? The Lord will teach him / He lights the pathways of all His Own //

He who fears God shall dwell in goodness / His Children shall inherit the Earth / His secret place is with His Servants / His Covenant shall bring a New Birth //

My eyes are fixed, are fixed on the Lord / He shall save me from Hell's plan for me / Turn toward me, have mercy on me, Lord / Desolate affliction take from me //

My heart is enlarged with my troubles / My soul signals a call of distress / Look kindly on all my affliction / Forgive my sins, and I will be blessed //

See my enemies, how they hate me? / With cruel designs they surround me / Keep my soul and deliver me / Keep me from shame, for I trust Thee //

Integrity and Righteousness / Keep me in the path of the blessed / I wait on You, Lord, all the day / Keep Israel from trouble's way

CHAPTER 26

"I Love to Linger in Your Holy House"

Keep me pure with righteous judgment, Oh my Lord / My footsteps have fallen upon honest places / I have placed my whole confidence in You, Lord / My footsteps shall follow the paths of Your Graces //

Look at all that lies within me, Oh my Lord / My decisions and all of my innermost heart / Your unfailing Kindness is in sight, Oh Lord / From Your Pathways of Truth I shall never depart //

I have not sat with vain people, Oh my Lord / I will not go in with those who cause dissention / I hate those who congregate to do evil / I will not join in with the wicked convention //

I will keep myself with all honesty / I will pray acceptable prayers in Your sight, Lord / I will tell of Your Great Love with thanksgiving / And publish Your Wonderful Works with great peace //

Lord, I love to linger in Your Holy House / And meditate upon Your Glory forever / Do not take away my soul with sinful men / Or let me lose my life through bloodthirsty violence //

Men of blood sow seeds of mischief with their hands / And they take bribes to subvert Your Equity / In integrity, I follow Your Commands / I seek Your Redemption, Lord, show me Your Mercy //

You have caused my feet to stand on solid ground / You gave me a safe place I could not afford / Everywhere I go, I raise the joyful sound / In all congregations will I bless the Lord

CHAPTER 27
"The Most Important Thing"

The Lord is my Guiding Light / And my Salvation / So I shall not fear / The Lord is my Source of Strength / Throughout my whole life / There is no fear here //

The wicked came upon me / All my enemies / They stumbled and fell / Though an army fight me / My heart shall not fear / The attacks of Hell //

The most important thing, Lord / The one thing I seek / To dwell in Your House / To behold Your Beauty, Lord / Throughout all my life / And to seek You out //

For in time of trouble / In His Pavilion / In His Secret Place / I know He shall hide me / His Tabernacle / The Rock, His Hiding Place //

I shall be above those / Who would oppress me / And so I shall sing / As I offer praises / Sacrifice to God / With joy to my King //

Oh Lord, please have mercy / Hear, and then answer / Your Face will I seek //

Please hide not Your Face, Lord / Do not forsake me / For You save the meek //

You will not forsake me / Father and Mother / May leave me down here / But You will take me / Teach me Your Way, Lord / My enemies fear //

I need a plain path, Lord / Enemies rise up / Their words are not true / Do not let them triumph / They speak out evil / I wait upon You //

My soul had fast fainted / But I believed You / Your Goodness is here / So have Godly courage / Your heart will be strong / Salvation is near

CHAPTER 28
"He Heard Me When I Cried"

I will cry unto the Lord / The Rock of my Salvation / Answer me, O still, small voice / And hear my supplication //

I will not go into the pit / Of Hell's disconsolation / Seeking Your Most Holy Face / Within Your Holy nation //

Workers of iniquity / Speak peace, but they are lying / They shall reap just what they sow / Because their souls are dying //

For not regarding the Lord / His handiwork they ignore / When the bill comes for their deeds / The price is set by the Lord //

He shall destroy their wicked souls / They shall not rise forever / But He heard me when I cried / The Lord shall leave me never //

God is my Strength and my Shield / The Lord helps those who trust Him / Now my heart is full of joy / With my song I will praise Him //

God gives strength to all His own / Who trust in His perfection / He gives His anointed ones / Provision and affection

CHAPTER 29
"God's Thunderous Voice"

Acknowledge the Lord's power / All you heavenly angels / Acknowledge God Almighty / Has all Power and Glory //

Acknowledge to the Lord all / Glory that is due to Him / Give worship to the Lord God / All splendorously Holy //
God's Thunderous Voice rules all / Rivers, lakes, seas and oceans / From the tiniest stream to / The vast, untamed deep waters //
God's Voice is omnipotent / And completely majestic / God's Thunderous Voice breaks the / Great Lebanon cedars //
Lebanon skips like a calf / Syria like a young ox / His fire and earthquakes have the / Kadesh wilderness flummoxed //
His Voice births deer and strips trees / So the forests are laid bare / All in His Temple cry Holy / In all the earth, He is there //
The Lord God is over the / Power of all floods and fires / Over all nations, tribes and tongues / God's Throne is much higher //
Forever the Lord God reigns / May His People all be strong / From His Conquering Robe's Train / They shall have peace all along

CHAPTER 30

"Joy Comes with the Morning Light"

Into Your Presence You have drawn me / You would not my foes rejoice in victory / For this I give You honor //
When I cried, Help, Lord, You did help me / You would not stop until You completely healed me / You have saved my soul from Hell //
When You restored me, You gave new life / Your anger subsided, You brought favor, not strife / For this I sing Your Praises //
Sing His Praises, O you saints of His / Give thanks to His Holy Name in all of your bliss / His anger gone, He blesses //
His anger is but for a short time / But the favor of the Lord lasts for a lifetime / Weeping endures for a night //
Even when the tears come down like rain / God's Children, His Own, know better than to complain / Joy comes with the morning light //
When Your blessings came, I realized / I shall not be moved from the Favor in Your Eyes / You made me strong on Favor's Mountain //
When You withdrew, my eyes cried tears, O Lord so great / In my dismay, I sought for mercy from Your Face / My soul was in a great strait //

How can You profit from my demise? / In the pit of death are none either strong or wise / None to tell your faithfulness //

Please hear, and show Your Mercy, Help me, / Please turn my mourning into joyous dancing, / From weeping to joyfulness //

You have loosed my sackcloth of sadness / Covered me with the linen robes of gladness / I will leave You nevermore //

And in the Praise of Your Salvation / I will sing of You throughout every nation / Give You glory evermore

CHAPTER 31
"My Spirit Belongs To You"

In You, Oh Lord, will I always place my trust / Free me from shame, deliver me in righteousness / Hear my prayer, Lord, and deliver speedily / Rock of Salvation, be the house of my defense //

For You, Oh Lord, are my Fortress and my Rock / Lead me and keep me from all my enemies / You are my Strength, my spirit beings to You / Your Truth keeps me from all the net they spread for me //

I hate the lips that speak lies and vanity / I trust You, Lord, and rejoice in all Your Mercy / You knew my troubles, saw my adversities, / You kept me from the hand of all my enemies //

You set me up a large room to worship Thee / I am in trouble, please have mercy upon me / My eyes with tears are consumed in all grief / My strength is gone because of my iniquity //

A laughingstock was I to my enemies / And all my neighbors took great pains to avoid me / Like a dead man out of sight and out of mind, / A sinking ship that all the sailors leave behind //

Many have slandered my name from every side / And tried to find the best way they could take my life / I trusted You, Lord, I said You were my God / Keep me, Oh Lord, from those who seek to bring me strife //

Let Your Face shine upon me for mercy's sake / I called upon You, do not let me be ashamed / Those wicked souls who have sought to hinder me / They will be silent, in the grave they cannot speak //

Those lying lips that contemptuously speak / Against the righteous, tell them all to hold their peace / Treasures of good things for all those who fear You / Shall be revealed, and just before the day is through //

You shall hide them from the eyes of evil men / In Your Pavilion, where they cannot get to them / Blessed be the Lord, for His kindness and defense / I thought that I was cut off from His recompense //

Your Eyes, Lord, saw me, and Your Ears heard my cry / Oh love the Lord, all of ye saints of His draw nigh / For He rewards all the faithful for all time / And brings revenge to all the evil for their crimes //

Be of good courage, Your heart can well afford / All of His Blessings, if your hope is in the Lord

CHAPTER 32

Surrounded by Mercy

The blessings of forgiveness for transgressions against God / Extend unto the covering of all sins man can see / The one to whom God imputes no iniquity is blessed / The one without deceitfulness is blessed abundantly //

Before the day that I confessed my sins, my bones waxed old / The springtime of my former state turned summer's drought so bold / So take a pause to reminisce on what this means to you / And sow in faith so you can reap a harvest that is true //

O Lord, I give acknowledgment of my iniquities / All my transgressions I confessed: You bore them all for me / So take a pause to reminisce on what this means to you / And sow in faith so you can reap a harvest that is true //

Since You forgave iniquities of my sins all around / All people will pray to You in a time Your Love abounds / In muddy, floody waters they in times of trial could drown / Outside the ark of safety where no refuge could be found //

You are my Hiding Place, O Lord, preserve me from trouble / Your Songs of all deliverance bless me on the double / So take a pause to reminisce on what this means to you / And sow in faith so you can reap a harvest that is true //

I am the Lord who teaches you and shows you how to go / And I will guide you with My Eye, I will lead, you follow / Do not be like the horse or mule, they do not understand / The bit and bridle hold them in lest they come at a man //

The wicked do not strive to know, they sorrow much, you see / Whoever trusts the Lord will be surrounded by mercy / So take a moment to be glad, and in the Lord rejoice / Your righteous, upright soul not sad, your heart will shout for joy

CHAPTER 33
"His Merciful Majesty"

Shout for joy, O righteous ones / Who keep your right standing with the Lord / Keep your heart with diligence / Praises beautify the upright soul //

Praise with psaltery and harp / Sing a praise song to the Lord / Sing to the Lord a new song / Play with great volume and great skill //

The Word of the Lord is right / His Works declare His True Faithfulness / Righteous judgment pleases Him / His Merciful Majesty rules all //

By His Word the heavens stand / The heavenly host is in His Hand / He scoops up the briny deep / Stores rivers, lakes, streams, oceans and seas //

Worship and revere the Lord / All who inhabit the Earth with awe / Bring your praises to the Lord / His Word is Gospel, His Word is Law //

The world stands, the heathen fall / Thoughts and plans against Him all fail / God's Counsel stands forever / His Heart and Thoughts will always prevail //

Blessed is that Godly nation / Whose people are God's Inheritance / The Lord looks down from Heaven / His Eyes see all the inhabitants //

He who makes all human hearts / Knows all of the things all people do / No king or mighty man stands / By horses or armies that march through //

The Lord's Eye is on His Own / Whose hearts fear the Lord and hope in Him / And His Lovingkindness reigns / To keep alive all who fear His Name //

Famine does not make us yield / God's Word is our Sword and Shield / Our heart shall rejoice in Him / And His Holy Name proclaim

CHAPTER 34
"I Will Bless the Lord at All Times"

I will bless the Lord at all times / I will speak and sing His Praises / I will boast in the Lord my God / The afflicted soul He raises //

O magnify the Lord with me / As together we lift Him here / I sought the Lord, He heard me / He delivered me from all fear //

They looked to Him and flowed to Him / And their countenance had no shame / This beggar cried, the Lord heard him / And took his troubles, Bless His Name //

The Angel of the Lord surrounds / Those who fear Him, and He saves them / O taste and see the Lord is good / Blessed are all those who trust in Him //

Give reverence to the Lord, saints / Those who revere Him shall not lack / The young lions thirst and hunger / His own know The Lord is not slack //

His Promises are right and true / I will prove why you should fear Him / Whatever He says, He will do / Heaven, Earth and Hell all fear Him //

Who desires long life and good things? / Speak no evil and no deceit / Run from evil, and go do good / Speak peace, and always pursue it //

The Lord sees and hears the righteous / He will come and quickly fix it / His wrath is toward evildoers / Their names He will disinherit //

The righteous cry, and the Lord hears / And delivers them from all trouble / The broken and contrite He loves / He will hear them on the double //

The righteous have afflictions, true / The Lord delivers from them all / He causes not one bone to break / Lest His Children stumble and fall //

The evil man from evil dies / The haters shall all be alone / The Redeemer of the soul lives / He will take care of all His Own

CHAPTER 35
"Plead My Case, Dear Lord"

Plead my case, dear Lord, / With those who war with me / Take the fight to them / Who take the fight to me //

Shield and Buckler be / To those who would help me / Bring Your spear to all / Who try to make me fall //

Savior of my soul / I need You to be whole / Let them be ashamed / Who try to take my life //

Let them be turned back / Confused, thrown off the track / Blow them in the wind / Send angels to chase them //

Let their way be dark / Cause their feet to slip / Persecute them, Lord / Who rigged for me a pit //

They set for me a net / Into it let them fall / I am joyful in You / Who saves me when I call //

All my bones rejoice / There is no one like You / The poor and needy wait / Deliverance is true //

False witnesses did rise / Their mouths were filled with lies / They did evil for good / Deprive my soul they would //

When they were sick, I prayed / In sackcloth I arrayed / My humble soul with fasting / Still they remained unchanged //

My prayer returned to me / Though I prayed earnestly / I bowed my soul in grief / As if for family //

In my adversity / They gathered against me / And though I knew it not / With hypocrites they mocked //

They feasted on my hurt / They gnashed their teeth in rage / Lord come to my rescue / When will You turn that page //

Obliterate their goal / And save my needy soul / To You I will give thanks / In the great congregation //

And I will praise Your Name / Among each tribe and nation / Hold back my enemies / Lest they falsely rejoice // Turn back conspiracies / They speak with warlike voice / They practice to deceive / The souls who live in peace //

They opened their mouths wide / In evil, deadly pride / To speak their vicious lies / Lord, speak, do not be quiet //

You have seen what they do / Lord, keep me close to You / Arise, Oh Lord, arise / With judgment by Your side //

Plead my case, dear Lord / My God, in You I hide / Judge me, Oh my God / By Your great righteousness //
Let not evil rejoice / To take away my soul / Do not let them say / We swallowed him up whole //
Let them be ashamed / Confusion fall like rain / On them who seek my hurt / Dishonor, shame them, Lord //
Let them shout for joy / With gladness in their voice / Who favor righteousness / And magnify Your Name //
Prosperity You give / In You my soul shall live / Your righteousness and praise / Forever I proclaim

CHAPTER 36

"*Your Unfailing Love*"

Transgression lies deep within the heart / It speaks evil within wicked man / Transgression makes evil men forget / The fear of God because of evil plans //
The evil man flatters himself much / He deceives himself with his pride and greed / He cannot bear to think he could be / Hated for deceit and iniquity //
He forsakes all that is wise or good / He makes evil plans at night in his bed / He seeks ill throughout his neighborhood / He hates no wrong until his day of death //
Your mercy, Lord, is in the heavens / Your faithfulness reaches into the clouds / Your righteousness is like great mountains / Your judgments deep as the ocean bounds //
You keep alive man and beast preserved / How excellent Your Unfailing Love / Extravagant, steadfast and faithful / On the wings of a peaceful white dove / (They know the abundance of Your House / Living water sent from up above) //
These waters are a fountain of life / Follow God's Light and you shall see light / Lord, keep Your Lovingkindness flowing / And Your Righteousness to the upright //
Keep me from the foot of pride and the / Hand of the wicked to remove me / The workers of iniquity fall / They are cast down and will rise no more

CHAPTER 37

"The Inheritance of the Meek"

Do not fret yourself because of evildoers / Do not envy the workers of iniquity / Soon they shall be cut down just as the tender grass / Soon they shall fade as the green herb in the sun's heat //

Trust in the Lord, and do good every day you live / Settle in, feed on faithfulness, delight in Him / He will give you the desires of your inner heart / Commit your way to the Lord, also trust in Him //

As you lean on the Lord, He will bring it to pass / He will bring forth your righteousness as the sunlight / And your justice as bright as the noonday sun's blast / As the Lord declares your work is right in His Sight //

Rest in the Lord, and be patient until He comes / Be still as you patiently wait on His Promise / Do not fret yourself when the wicked man prospers / Cease from anger, wrath and evil which rob your bliss //

Those who do evil shall be cut off from the Lord / But the Earth is the inheritance of the meek / In just a little while, the wicked shall not be / Though you search diligently, yet he shall not be //

But the Earth is the inheritance of the meek / The meek shall delight themselves in abundant peace / The wicked man plots against the righteous, and he / Gnashes his teeth, but the Lord laughs at evil deeds //

The Lord knows his day is coming, even though the / Wicked have drawn out their sword, bent their bow to cast / Down the poor and needy, and to slay the upright / Their sword shall pierce their heart, their bows break, they shall pass //

The little the righteous man has is better than / Treasures of wicked arms that soon the Lord shall break / The enemies of the Lord soon shall be consumed / But the earth is the inheritance of the meek //

For the Lord knows the days that the righteous ones face / So He gives their inheritance forevermore / They shall not be ashamed when the evil days come / When famine comes, they shall have an abundant store //

But the wicked shall be as a burnt offering / In the day the Lord takes away their precious things / They shall be as a ram or a lamb sacrificed / In the day that they enter the smoke and the flame //

The wicked man borrows, but never pays it back / But the righteous shows mercy and gives without slack / Those who are blessed of Him shall inherit the Earth / They that be cursed of Him shall be cut off in dearth //

The steps of a good man are established by God / When He delights in his way, He keeps all his steps / Even when he falls, the Lord shall not cast him down / For the Lord lifts him up in His Hand, he won't slip //

I once was young, but now I am an older man / Yet I have never seen the righteous forsaken / Nor have I ever seen his children begging bread / He is ever Merciful, and lends, and blesses //

Stay away from the evil and cling to the good / And your life will forever be safe and secure / For the Lord loves good judgment and keeps all His Saints / Though the wicked be cut off, your life shall endure //

The righteous shall inherit the land forever / Those who are consistently righteous shall never leave / The righteous speaks wisdom, and his tongue speaks justice / God's Law in his heart will not let him secede //

The wicked lie in wait to kill off the righteous / The Lord will not leave him to be judged and condemned / Wait on the Lord, keep His way, He will exalt you / When the wicked are cut off, you shall see it then //

I have seen a wicked man when he has great power / Flourishing like a green shade tree in its hometown / But the next time I passed, he was no longer there / I searched and asked for him, but he could not be found //

Observe the pure person, and behold the upright / There is a posterity for the man of peace / And the transgressors shall be destroyed together / And the posterity of the wicked shall cease //

But the Salvation of the righteous is the Lord's / He is their stronghold in the time of their hiding / He rescues them and delivers them from trouble / From wicked men, for in Him they are abiding

CHAPTER 38
"My Hope is in You"

Oh Lord, please do not rebuke me in anger / Or send Your discipline when You are enraged / Your arrows have struck me and now they are stuck / Your heavy hand presses as though I am caged //

There is no soundness in me through Your anger / Because of sin, my whole body is sick / For my iniquities loom over my head / They are a burden too heavy and thick //

My wounds ooze corruption because of my foolishness / I am bent and bowed down as I mourn all day long / My body is sick with an undisclosed illness / My bruised, anguished heart makes me moan loud and strong //

Lord, You know all my longing and sighing and crying / You know my every thought and desire / I am bruised, torn and tattered, my heart throbs within me / And the light in my eyes has become a dim fire //

My friends and companions stand far from my plague / Even my closest friends keep themselves far from me / My enemies set traps, say false, malicious things / They think up lies and deceit just for me //

But I'm like the deaf man who hears not a sound / And like the deaf mute, I will say not a word / Just like the deaf man, I pretend not to hear / Because my defenses are all too absurd //

All my hope is in You, Lord, Your Answer will come / For I pray, Lord, do not let them gloat over me / Who would magnify themselves if my foot should slip / For I am close to falling, pain is constant with me //

I confess my guilt and am sorry for my sin / But my enemies are all quite lively and strong / Those who wrongfully hate me have increased in number / They repay good with evil, for right they do wrong //

Don't abandon me, Lord, my God, stay close beside me / Please come quickly to help me, my Lord and my God / For you are my sword and my shield, my salvation / Please come quickly to help me, my Lord and my God

CHAPTER 39
"What Time I Have Here"

I said to myself, I will watch what I do / I will not sin against You by what words I say / I said to myself, I will bridle my mouth / While the wicked man speaks of his evil all day //

I held back my tongue, didn't say good or bad / And I felt so much sorrow, such trouble I had / My heart burned within as I listened to him / Then I spoke with my tongue, I could not hold it in //

Lord, help me to know the end of all my days / and I really must know now what time I have here / I know that You know just how weak that I am / And my days as an hand breadth are drawing quite near //

All riches of mankind are just a vain shadow / They trouble themselves just to make a great name / The riches of rich men stay not with themselves / They heap treasure, not knowing who gathers them //

And what do I wait for? My hope is in You / Take me far away from all my secret sins / Don't make me a laughingstock of wicked men / Deliver me from my transgressions within //

I spoke not a word because You made it so / And I was consumed by Your powerful Hand / Iniquity mars the whole beauty of man / His beauty is ashes when You rebuke him //

Take all the time you need to understand this / Please hear me and answer and give favor too / A stranger and foreigner from a long line / Help me gain my strength before my life is through

CHAPTER 40
"Your Will, My God, is My Delight"

I waited for You, Oh my Lord / With patience, and You came / Intently You heard all my words, / My cry unto Your Name //

You brought me from a devil's den / Out of the miry clay / You gave stability within / And guided all the way //

You put a new song in my mouth / And I will praise my God / And those who hear my song will fear / And trust upon the Lord //

The man who makes the Lord his trust / And puts away his pride / Will find the blessing of the Lord / Deliverance from lies //

The many works that You have done / And wonders will not cease / Your thoughts toward Your children / None can reckon unto Thee //

If I attempt to tell them all / They're more than could be told / Though my tongue were a ready pen / With words of finest gold //

I brought my sacrifice to You / My Lord, My God, My King / Your words dug deep into my ears / More than an offering //

Burnt offering You did not seek / Nor offering for sin / You said to come just as foretold / My offering within //

Your Will, my God, is my delight / Your Law is in my heart / I have not ceased from preaching truth / Your right ways to impart //

My lips were not sealed, O my Lord / Within my righteous heart / Your Lovingkindness and Your Truth / In whole, not just in part //

Please keep not back Your Mercies, Lord / Your Lovingkindness keep / And Your Eternal Truth, O Lord / Continually keep me //

For evil has surrounded me / Because of all my sins / Iniquities have me downcast / I can't look up again //

They are too much for me to count / My heart leaves me for dead / Please come quick to deliver me / O Lifter of my head //

Let shame's confusion seek the death / Of those who seek my soul / Please drive them back, put them to shame / Let not evil control //

Give them a desolate reward / Who shamefully accuse / Let all who seek the Lord rejoice / With joy at Your Good News //

Let those who love salvation say / The Lord be magnified / Who gives salvation day to day / His goodness to arrive //

But I am poor and needy, Lord / Yet You think upon me / My help and my deliverer / My God, please come quickly

CHAPTER 41

"Be Merciful Unto Me, O Lord"

There is a blessing unto the man / Who sees to the poor and sick and weak / There is deliverance for that man / In the evil day, preserves the meek //

The Lord will keep him alive and blessed / He will not fall to his enemies / God gives strength to him when he is sick / The Lord turns him from sick to healthy //

I saw the Lord's Goodness and I cried / Heal my soul, I have sinned against Thee / My enemies ask, When will he die? / They wish no more influence for me //

And if perchance they make a visit / Vain lies and iniquity they bring / They serve themselves within all their hearts / And then they go tell an evil thing //

Those who hate me whisper against me / A campaign of lies to seek my hurt / An evil end they claim against me / They say, He will not rise from the dirt //

Even my trusted friend turned his back / He who ate of my bread wished me dead / Your mercy can show them their error / For You are the Lifter of my head //

Because You give favor unto me / I fall not before my enemies / You keep me in my integrity / Forever my face is before Thee //

The Lord God of Israel be blessed / Everlasting to everlasting / From the beginning to the ending / Your people say Amen and Amen

CHAPTER 42
"The Depressed, Disheartened Soul"

As the deer cries and pants for water / So pants my soul after You, O God / My soul pants for God, the Living God / When shall my soul appear before God? //

I have watered the ground with my tears / Day and night they cry, Where is your God? / My soul is poured out like waterfalls / As the multitude turns before God //

With praise and worship at Holy Day / Why be the depressed, disheartened soul? / I trust God, hope in Him, still praise Him / Who shines His Countenance in my soul //

O my God, my soul looks down in me / Because of this, I will remember / How in Jordan You looked down on me / From a mountaintop I remember //

In the land where the Hermonites dwell / Upon the little hill of Mizar / Deep calls to deep where Your Waterspouts' / Waves and Billows go over my heart //

In the day, You show Lovingkindness / In the night, You give a song of life / My song and prayer are unto You, Lord / You will be my God all of my life //

I will say to God who is my Rock / Why have You forgotten me today? / Why do I mourn when oppression comes / Like an enemy sword every day? //

Like a killing field they reproach me / Every day they ask, Where is your God? / Why be the depressed, disheartened soul? //

I trust God, hope in Him, still praise Him / Who shines His Countenance on my soul / My health and countenance are from God

CHAPTER 43
"Your Light and Your Truth"

Judge me, O God, and plead my case now / Against an unmerciful nation / Save me from deceitful injustice / You are the God of my salvation //

Why would You cast me off from this place? / Why must I mourn the oppression here? / O Lord, send out Your Light and Your Truth / Lead me into Your Most Holy Place //

Then will I offer on Your Altar / Sacrifices of joy and of praise / On the harp will I praise You, my God / You are Lord God of all, O my God //

Why be the depressed, disheartened soul? / I trust God, hope in Him, still praise Him / Who shines His Countenance on my soul / My health and countenance are from God

CHAPTER 44
"We Have Heard About You"

We have heard about You / And what You do / O God, what marvelous things You have done! //

You took out the heathen / Put Your People in / You sent a cruel message / Against evil men //

Your People did not fight / Or show their own might / Your Power and Glory and Light saved them //

You are my king, O God / Deliverance bring / By Your Name, we tread down our enemies //

My bow cannot save me / My sword will not save / You crush our enemies / And put them to shame //

Our boast is in You, Lord / And we praise Your Name / Think on this! But when You cast us away, //

You have sent us dismay / If You forsake us / They that hate us will take / Their spoils of war //

You have made us like sheep / Appointed for meat / You have scattered our name / Among the profane //

You have sold us for naught / With no profit sought / A scorn and laughingstock to our neighbors //

They shake their heads and roar / Tell stories, and more / I stand confused, ashamed, / As they blaspheme //

They have reproached Your Name / The enemy came / To take revenge for all his battles lost //

This has come upon us / But in You we trust / We are true to Your Word / Our prayers You have heard //

And our heart beats for You / To You we are true / Though You have broken us where dragons roar //

In the shadow of death / With our fleeting breath / If we forget Your Name in false worship //

You will search this all out / You know it by now / We are killed all day long / And we are not strong //

We are slaughtered like sheep / O Lord, do not sleep / It seems You have cast us off forever //

Why would You hide Your Face / In an oppressed place? / You know our frame is weak and afflicted //

I am bowed to the earth / My soul is in dearth / My body is bowed down / It touches the ground //

Arise for the Lord's Help / Man cannot give help / And please redeem us for Your Mercy's sake //

We have heard about You / And what You can do / So please redeem us for Your Mercy's sake

CHAPTER 45
"The King's Daughter"

My heart is telling a story of love / The qualities of my King from above / My tongue expounds a worthy narrative //

Your Glory is greater than other men / The grace of Your Speech is sealed from within / God's Blessing on you will last forever //

The sword of judgment is upon Your Thigh / Your Majesty glorious, O Lord Most High / Ride on in truth, righteousness and meekness //

Your Right Hand of power does wondrous things / Your Enemies fall by Your Arrow's stings / Those who oppose You fall by Your Power //

Your Throne shall forever and ever stand / The scepter of Your Kingdom in Your Hand / You love uprightness and hate wickedness //

The oil of gladness God has poured upon You / Others cannot do the things that You do / Myrrh, aloes and cassia fragrance You //

From ivory palaces the King plays / Stringed instruments and harps to give God praise / The fragrance of his worship makes You glad //

The King has many daughters of honor / Your Queen beside you in gold of Ophir / O King's Daughter, listen, and consider //

Incline your ear, and live unto your King / Give heed unto the instruction he brings / Your life that is past shall be left behind //

The King will see your beauty and grace / Obey, revere Him, and seek His Face / Through all your days, give honor to Him //

Other king's daughters seek your favor / Riches shall find you from your neighbor / As they entreat your beautiful face //

The King's Daughter is full of glory / Her gold-inlaid robe tells the story / In fine needlework she sees the King //

Her righteous companions follow near / Her virtuous virgins, O so dear / With her maidens, she comes before Thee //

With joy and gladness they shall come near / Into your palace with Godly Fear / Your children shall rule over the Earth //

O King's Daughter, your name shall be praised / All generations shall have it raised / Forever you shall live in honor

CHAPTER 46
"When Comes the Morning"

God is our Hiding Place and our Source of Strength / He is always there in the time of trouble / In earthquake or tsunami we shall not fear / In floodwaters or when the mountains tremble / Stop and think on that for awhile //

There is a healing river whose streams make glad / The New Jerusalem come down from Heaven / Its healing waters serve the Most Holy Place / Of the earthly tabernacles God-given //

The river of God which flows to that city / Shall never be moved, but flows when comes the morning / The heathen raged against this river of joy / Dark kingdoms raged until the Lord uttered His Voice //

The nations drank from the refreshing water / Then the Lord spoke, and the Earth melted away / The Lord of Heaven, Earth and Hell / Is with us here today / Because He is our Hiding Place / We shall not flee away / Stop and think on that for awhile //

Nobody can cause desolation like God / He stops wars, breaks bows, and cuts spears in two / He burns chariots in a flame of fire / He cries, Be still, and know that I am God //

My Name shall be known among all the heathen / I shall be exalted in all of the Earth / He is the Lord of Hosts, and He is with us / The God of Jacob is our refuge on earth / Stop and think on that for awhile

CHAPTER 47
"Sing Praises"

Clap your hands, all ye people / Give to God a triumphant shout / The Lord Most High is awesome / This the whole world shall soon find out //

He shall subdue the nations / Many people under our feet / Our inheritance is His / The sons of Jacob at His Seat //

Meditate upon this truth //

With a shout, God arises / The trumpet of the Lord shall sound //

Sing praises to God, Praise Him / Sing praises to our King, Praise Him / God is King of all the Earth / With understanding, Sing His Praises //

God rules the heathen nations / His Holiness brings salvation // Leaders from all of the Earth / With the people of Abraham / God is their Shield and Defender / Let us exalt the Great I AM

CHAPTER 48

"Take a Walk About Zion"

The Lord is great, praiseworthy above all / Within the city gates on the Holy Mountain / Beautifully situated, and joyful / On the North Face of the Mountain of Zion //
Within the Palaces of the King of Kings / God is famous for giving refuge to all / Many kings assembled to make a great war / When they passed The City, the assembly was called //
They saw it together, with all its bulwarks / They marveled at its power, and were soon troubled / In fear, they hastened to depart from that place / As a woman in labor, they greatly travailed //
You broke the ships of Tarshish with an east wind / We have heard and seen the strength of That City / It is the City of the Lord God of Hosts / The Almighty God is the Strength of That City //
God will establish The City forever / Take some time to reflect upon this joyful thought / We have thought about Your Love in the Temple / Your Lovingkindness is known among Your People //
Your Name is to be praised among the whole Earth / Your Righteous Power causes Zion to rejoice / The daughters of Judah rejoice in Your Truths / Your Judgments give cause for the people to rejoice //
Take a walk about Zion, go around her / Tell all the towers and mark all the bulwarks there / Consider her palaces, talk about it / The world really needs to hear what happened there //
This God is our God forever and ever / Forever He shall guide us in life and in death

CHAPTER 49
"Speaking of Wisdom"

Hear ye, Hear ye, all ye people / Lend me your ears, ye inhabitants of the world / Men of low estate or high place / Whether rich or poor, this message is still unfurled //

Speaking of wisdom, I shall speak / My heart shall meditate on ways to understand / I will listen to parables / I will keep my meditation with songs at hand //

Why should I fear the evil days / Even when it seems evil things surround the good / People who trust in their money / Or boast how they can use their money to do good //

Not one can redeem his brother / No matter how much ransom is offered to God / The soul's redemption is precious / There is nothing he can do to turn the clock //

So his brother could live forever without sin / Both wise and foolish in the grave / The substance of their increase goes to other men / Who call their lands by their own names //

They think their house is for always / And their dwelling places to all generations / Though their lives are filled with honors / Men, like beasts, perish throughout all the nations //

Their families mark all they say / Pause to meditate on these words / Like sheep, they are laid in the grave / As they are laid to rest, others control their works //

Beauty is destroyed in the grave / But God shall redeem me from the power of the grave / He shall receive me to Himself / Pause to meditate on these words //

Do not fear when one attracts wealth / When the substance of his household is made richer / When he dies, he leaves it all behind / The glory of his riches cannot follow after //

He is a blessing to himself / And others will give blessings to a man of wealth / In death he leaves it all behind / When he dies, he leaves behind his wealth //

He will be laid by his fathers / Both he and his ancestors will lie in darkness / Honor without understanding / Makes the man like a beast, buried in darkness

CHAPTER 50
"A Double Order"

The Mighty God has spoken / The Lord has called the Earth / From the rising to the setting of the Sun / The Lord God of perfection / Creator of beauty / Has shined His Light on the Earth from Mount Zion //

The Lord will not keep silence / A fire devours before Him / From the time of His Coming the tempest roars / He shall call to the heavens / Also, He shall call the Earth / He shall then judge His Children forevermore //

Gather my saints around me / Who have daily sacrificed / And the heavens will proclaim His Righteousness / God is the Judge of all / Think upon His Sacrifice / Not of bulls, or of goats, but a contrite heart //

Hear my call, O Israel / And I will speak unto you / I am the Lord who testifies against you / Sacrifice, burnt offerings / Bullocks or he goats for me / None of these do I come to require from you //

The beasts of the field are mine / The cattle, fowl and wild beasts / If I were hungry, I would never tell you / The fullness of Earth is mine / I own each bird and each beast / Should I entreat for bulls or goats from you //

Offer thanksgiving to me / Pay your vows unto the Lord / Call, and I will answer and deliver / In the day of trouble / Do not cease to call on me / I will save, and you will praise me ever //

A word to the wicked / What have you to do with me / My statutes and my covenant you hate / My instruction and words / You soon cast out behind you / To thieves and adulterers you relate //

Slanders and evil lies / You speak, and vouch for others / You even speak against your own brothers / When I did not answer, / You thought that I was like you / I will rebuke and expose all you do //

You who forget me, hear ye / If I visit you in rage / I will tear you so none can repair you / Those who praise me give glory / A double order is due / Those who walk and talk right I will save

CHAPTER 51
"Create a Clean Heart in Me"

I need Your Mercy to rain down on me, O God / Because of Your Unfailing Love / It is Your Nature to show multiple mercies / To prove Your Kindness from above //

I know if You cleanse me thoroughly from my sin / You will wash my iniquity / I know right well that I have transgressed against You / My sin is always before me //

I have sinned and done evil in Your Sight alone / You are clearly just against me / Before I was born, I inherited sin's curse / In which my mother conceived me //

You desire that Your Truth would reign on the inside / From Your Wisdom I cannot hide / Purify me outside with hyssop to cleanse me / Wash me inside like snow pure white //

Create a clean heart in me as only You can / Help my spirit form a new man / Whatever You do, please do not cast me away / I need Your Presence every day //

Please restore to me the joy of Your Salvation / Lift my willing spirit today / Then I will teach the transgressors Your Ways, O Lord / Many sinners will come Your Way //

Keep me from violent bloodthirstiness, O God / You are God of my salvation / And I shall sing aloud of all Your Righteousness / Your Praise to every nation //

You do not ask for sacrifices I would bring / You do not need burnt offerings / A broken spirit is the thing that You require / A contrite heart you will take higher //

Do good in Your Good Pleasure to Mount Zion, Lord / Build the walls of Jerusalem / Righteous sacrifices and burnt offerings / Will be pleasing unto You then

CHAPTER 52
"He Who Trusted in His Own Strength"

Why do you brag about the bad you do? / O strong man, the goodness of God is before you / Your evil tongue thinks about bad always / Like a sharp razor, it cuts out the righteous ways / And you would rather do evil than good / And lie when the truth would be better understood / Think about this for awhile //

You love devouring words of deceit / You who destroy, destruction shall be your meat / God shall destroy you forevermore / He shall take you away from where you live / From the land of the living where you live / You shall see that land of the living nevermore / Think about this for awhile //

When the righteous see this, they shall fear God / They shall laugh at him who did not make God his strength / He who trusted in his own strength and might / And boldly made wickedness the source of his strength //

But I shall bear fruit as the olive tree / I will trust in the Mercy of God forever / I will praise You for all You did for me / I will praise Your Name with all the saints evermore

CHAPTER 53

"They Never Called on God"

The declarations of a fool's heart / Deny the existence of God / Corruption and abomination / Do not let him do any good //

God searched to find some understanding / People that would seek after Him / They turned aside from Godly fearing / To fear the Lord is not in them //

The evildoers have no knowledge / They eat up my people like bread / There is not even one that does good / They never called on God instead //

They feared a fear where there was no fear / Their bones were scattered in defeat / They camped against the people of God / Their wealth became His Children's Meat //

The Lord has despised the hearts of pride / But we seek salvation from Zion / When God turns Israel's captivity / The sons of Jacob rejoice

CHAPTER 54
"God is the Source of My Help"

I plead my salvation by Your Name / And ask for good judgment by Your Strength / Hear my prayer, give ear to my words, Lord / For strangers come to war against me //
Oppressors come to destroy my soul / They have not sought after Your Great Name //
May God's Children pause to reflect upon this //
I know God is the Source of my help / The Lord helps all those who uphold me / Evil shall befall my enemies / Who seek not the truth that sets men free //
I will bring my sacrifice to You / And praise Your Name, Lord, for it is good / You have saved me out of all trouble / Won the battle as only You could //
My eyes have seen all Your Heart's Desire / Against Your enemies by Your Power

CHAPTER 55
"The Prayer of the Betrayed"

Please give ear to my petition, O God / And stay close by while I give my request / Give Your Attendance and Understanding / I cry aloud because of grievousness //
The enemy and the oppressors roar / They ascribe evil intent unto me / They hate all that I love, my heart grieves sore / Deadly fear, trembling and horror stalk me //
If I had the wings of a snow-white dove / I would fly away to a place of rest / In the wilderness of obscurity / I would escape from the storm and tempest //
Please take time to think about this //
Please hand the enemy a sound defeat / Destroy and confuse their violent strife / Day and night they attack from all sides now / They strive to bring sadness and loss of life //
Wicked souls are behind all of this war / Subterfuge and bitterness form their plan / If it had been my enemy's dark plan / One who hated me, I could understand //

I could have borne that and found a safe place / But it was my friend, a man of my grade / We walked together in the House of God / The prayer of the betrayed is what I prayed //

Let Death and Hell be quick to overtake / For everything they touch turns wicked / I will call the Lord, and the Lord will hear / Morning, noon, and night, and the Lord will hear //

He has kept me in peace from the battle / More there were with me than the enemy / God has heard my cry, and will afflict him / God whose Throne is high in the heavenlies //

Please take pause to think about this //

Because God has not set His Swift Judgment / The workers of iniquity fear Him not / The enemy did break His Covenant / By killing peaceful men, they earned a blot //

The words of his mouth were smooth as drawn butter / But the enemy kept war in his heart / Softer than the softest oil were his speeches / But his intent was a fiery dart //

Wrap your gifts and place them at God's Altar / Place Him first, and He shall give you sustenance / Those who serve the righteous God are righteous / He shall keep in place their joyful countenance //

But You, O Lord, shall send their destruction / Those who live by violence shall surely die / Men of blood and deceit are soon quite gone / But I will trust in the Name of the Lord Most High

CHAPTER 56

"I Have Placed My Trust in the Lord"

O God, have mercy on me / My enemies would swallow me / they fight daily to oppress me / My enemies would devour me //

Many rise to fight against me / I will not let fear conquer me / But put instead my trust in Thee / I will praise the Word of the Lord //

I have placed my trust in the Lord / I will not fear what man can do / They change the meaning of my words / Their evil fights both me and You //

They congregate to plan evil / They lurk in hiding for my soul / Can they get by with their evil? / Lord, cast down the evil people //

You know everywhere that I hide / You put my tears in a bottle / In Your Book are they not inside? / Turn back my foes in the battle //

When I cry to You, You shall rise / My foes flee, for You are with me / I will praise the Word of my God / I will praise the Word of the Lord //

I have placed my trust in the Lord / I will not fear what man can do / My vows to the Lord are with me / I render my praise unto Thee //

You have delivered me from death / You shall keep my feet from falling / I shall forever walk with God / Within the land of the living

CHAPTER 57

"A Fixed Heart on Your Glory"

Show Your Mercy to me, Lord, show Your Mercy to me / My soul trusteth in Thee, Lord, my soul trusteth in Thee / And my refuge shall be in the shadow of Your Wings / Until the storm is over with no calamity //

In the storms of affliction will I cry to Thee / You are the Lord Most High who performs these things for me / In the floods of reproach, Heaven's Angels save me / From the reproach of him who would love to swallow me //

Think about this and praise the Lord who sits on His Throne //

My soul is set down among the lions of the chase / In the fires of division, I must run my race / Men whose teeth are spears and arrows, and their tongue a sword / They can only be defeated by the Living Lord //

Be lifted up, Mighty God, above all the heavens / Let Your Glory shine, Living Lord, above all the Earth / They have fixed a net to try to cause my steps to fall / My soul is bowed to the ground, Lord, to You I call //

They have rigged a pit to swallow me whole, head to toes / In the quicksand of opposition fall my foes //

Think about this and praise the Lord who sits on His Throne //

I have a fixed heart on Your Glory, O Lord, my God / I have prepared to sing and to give You praises / I will stir up the gift in me to give You praises / Psaltery and harp will sound early, O Lord, my God //

I will show forth Your Glory among all the people / I will sing praises to You among all the nations / For Your Mercy extends all the way to the heavens / And Your Truth from the grave to the earth to the high clouds //

Let Your Praise, O God, be lifted above the heavens / And let Your Glory be raised above all the whole Earth

CHAPTER 58
"Strangers to Righteousness"

Do you in all truth speak righteousness, O congregation? / Do you judge matters in fairness, O you sons of men? / From the belly you do wicked works all the day long / You weigh violence to see how much you can get in //

The wicked are strangers to righteousness before they are born / From birth they have ability the truth to suborn / Their poison is like the poison of an adder gone stone deaf / Which hears not the snake charmer's song, but strikes him to death //

Great cunning is no defense for the snake charmer thus stricken / Lord, take these evil ones and let their teeth be broken / Break out the teeth of the young lions and they shall be broken / As disappearing rainwaters, let them be smitten //

When the enemy archer bends his bow, strike down his soul / As the slug vanishes away, so let them all melt / As the premature birth makes the baby to be stillborn / Take them alive, as a whirlwind, have them thus dealt //

Before the sound of thorns which strike the pot as it boils down / The righteous shall rejoice to know judgment is found / The righteous wash their feet in the blood of the wicked / So that men will say there is a reward for the righteous //

Truly the true God will judge on His Throne in the earth

CHAPTER 59
"Be My Defense"

Be my deliverance, O my God, from all my enemies / Be my defense, O Lord, from those who rise against me / Be my deliverance from the workers of iniquity / Be my salvation, O Lord Most High, from all bloody men //

For the workers of iniquity lie in wait for my soul / And lo, the mighty, evil ones come to take control / Not because of sin that I have done, or some transgression bold / But they run to prepare for a battle with no cause //

Meet me where I cry unto You, and behold the things they do / Meet me, O Lord God of Hosts, where I cry unto You / Rain down Your Punishment to the nations that will not serve You / To all the evil, terroristic people, spare not //

Stop to reflect upon this truth, and the mighty Hand of God / They bring their evil wickedness out after nightfall / They snarl like a dog and run about the city walls / Fire breathes from their mouths and warfare from their lips calls //

For they are convinced that the Lord cannot hear their roar / O Lord God of my strength, I will wait upon Thee / For God is my defense and the God of my mercy / The God of my mercy shall come see about me //

God will let me gaze in triumph on my enemies / Do not kill them, Lord, lest Your People soon forget / Let them wander place to place as Your Victory sets / Then bring them down, O Lord, our Shield and Protector //

Trap them in pride, the curses they curse and lies they lie / Consume them in wrath again and until they die / They shall know the God of Jacob rules Earth from on High / Stop to reflect on this truth, and the mighty Hand of God //

Let them snarl like a dog and run about the city / Let them wander around the length of the town in search of meat / Let them stay inside the city through the night, hungry / Let them feel the sting of their unsuccessful journey //

But I will sing of Your Power and Mercy always / In the morning will I declare Your Goodness each day / You have been my defense and refuge in troublous days / I will sing unto You, my Strength, Defense and Mercy //

All these things come from You, You are the God of my Strength / You are the God of my Defense, God of my Mercy

CHAPTER 60
"Please Turn to Us Again"

O God, we have become castaways / You have scattered us, displeased with our ways / Please turn to us again //

You have made Earth a place of trembling / Please repair it, for it is collapsing / You have shown us hard things //

You gave us wine of astonishment / We staggered under this astonishment / Please help us recover //

You have given the banner of Truth / To the people who fear You every day / We must display Your Truth //

Selah. / Your beloved must be delivered / By Your saving Hand You will deliver //

Save and deliver, Lord / God has spoken in His Holiness / I will rejoice when I divide Shechem //

Line out Succoth Valley / Gilead and Manasseh are Mine / Ephraim is the helmet on My Head //

Judah is My Scepter / Moab is My Washpot, Edom is / The place I cast My Shoe //

Philistia, triumph over me / Who will lead me into the strong city? / Who will lead me into Edom? //

Isn't it You, O God? / Even though You made us castaways / And did not go with our armies //

Give us help with troubles / Man cannot help, but God is able / Through God we shall defeat our enemies

CHAPTER 61
"Lead Me to the Rock"

Hear me when I cry, O God, listen to my prayer / From one end of the Earth to the other I cry / I will call on You when my heart is overwhelmed / Lead me to the Rock that is much higher than I //

You have been my source of shelter and my strong tower / Your tabernacle hides me from my enemy / The covert of Your Wings is my hiding place ever / I shall meditate upon Your Tender Mercies //

You have heard the vows that I have vowed unto You / I am in the heritage of those who fear You / I know that you shall extend my life many years / You add generations to the days of the king // The king abides ever in the Presence of God / Mercy and Truth are the preservatives therein / Therefore will I sing praises to God forever / Praising Your Name as I vow to You for my sins

CHAPTER 62

"The Excellency of My Expectation"

My soul waits on God, the Source of Revelation / My God alone is my Rock and my Salvation / With God as my Defender, I shall not be moved //
O evil ones, how long do you plot evil deeds? / As a sagging wall or shaking fence, so are ye / They despise the excellency of His Goodness //
Lies are the source of the evil ones' delight / They love to bless by day and then curse by night / Pause to consider the power of this truth //
O my soul, wait only on God my Salvation / The Excellency of my expectation / My God alone is my Rock and my Salvation //
With God as my Defender, I shall not be moved / My salvation and glory and strength, my refuge / Lies within the God in whom I trust at all times //
Always trust Him and pour your heart out to Him / Oh //
My people, we can take refuge in Him / Pause to consider the power of this truth //
Low men are vain, and high men know how to lie / Put them side by side, and they are all alike / Oppression and robbery do not make rich //
If riches increase by them, be not deceived / God spoke once, then twice, Power belongs to Me / Not only power belongs to Thee, Lord //

But also mercy belongs to Thee, Lord / For in every work mankind affords / You render to each one accordingly

CHAPTER 63
"I Will Seek You Early"

God, You are my God, I will seek You early / In this wilderness my soul and flesh are parched and dry / Barren land cries for Your Power and Glory / In Your House I have seen You and therefore do I cry //

For Your Lovingkindness is better than life / I praise You with willing lips for as long as I live / I lift holy hands that I might bless Your Name / With marrow and fatness I praise You with joyful lips //

My soul is satisfied when I consider / When I meditate upon You in the night / My help and protection are in Your Shadow / Therefore will I rejoice with the morning light //

My soul is following on hard to know You / My heart clings to You, and Your Right Hand upholds me / Those who seek to destroy me shall know the grave / Jackals dine on them, the sword shall be their meat //

But the king shall ever rejoice in the Lord / All who fear the Lord shall have cause to glory / But the mouths of the evil, lying people / Shall be silenced by the Lord God Almighty

CHAPTER 64
"Just One of His Arrows"

My prayer is continually active before You / Oh God, hear my voice and preserve my life from fear / From the secret plans of the wicked ones hide me / From the insurrection of sinners, hide me here //

They whet their tongues and bend their bows with bitter words / Like a sniper, they shoot at the just with no pause / They encourage one another to do evil in the dark / God will shoot them with just one of his arrows //

In their wounded state, they shall turn on one another / All who see their treachery shall flee far away from them / In their fear, men shall declare the wondrous Works of God / For they shall see what God can do to others and to them //

As for the righteous soul, he shall rejoice in God / And shall place his trust in Him continually / And all the upright in heart shall see the Lord's Work / As day by day they declare His Grace and Glory

CHAPTER 65
"Sunrise Service and Sunset Praises"

In Zion, praise is preparing for You, Oh God / And today, vows will be performed unto You, Lord / You hear every prayer, and to You all living creatures come / Actions of my guilt are expunged from Your Record //

Those who are chosen to approach to Your Courtyards, / We are enraptured by the goodness of Your House / We shall be renewed in Your Holy Nation / With awesome deeds, You will show Your Salvation //

You are the One the whole world will have faith in / From the ends of the Earth to the distant shores / Your Majesty spoke the mountains into being / The roaring seas, the crashing waves praise You, Lord //

The tumultuous people praise you with seas and waves / You calm the seas, still the waves, and heal the tumult / From the ends of the earth, the people stand in awe / Sunrise service and sunset praises will exalt //

When the earth cries for rain, You answer with water / You send liquid blessing from the River of God / You provide grain and prepare the earth for water / You drench the furrows and soak up the ground, Oh God //

You fill the ridges and bring the spring showers to Earth / The ridges flowing, the spring showers bringing new birth / You crown the year with good things, and Your Paths drop richness / The goodness of Your Year extends into the wilderness //

All the little hills rejoice with goodness all around / Healthy flocks fill the countryside on the verdant ground / Rows and rows of healthy corn bring the valley gladness / The people shout and sing, for there is no more sadness

CHAPTER 66
"The Joyful Sound of Praise"

Make a joyful shout unto God / All the Earth, sing His Glory / The glory due to His Great Name / So make His Praise glorious //

Oh God, how awesome are Your Works / Your Power shows Your Greatness / Because of Your Omnipotence / Your enemies must obey //

All the Earth will worship You, Lord / All the Earth will sing to You / All the Earth will sing to Your Name / Pause to think what God can do //

Come and see the things God has done / Awesome works toward all mankind / He turned the sea into dry land / They crossed to the other side //

The enemy drowned in the sea / Thy people rejoiced in Thee / He rules by His Hand forever / All the world is in His view / Let no rebel be exalted / Pause to think what God can do //

Oh bless the Lord, all ye people / Sing the joyful sound of praise / He preserves our lives and purpose / Mighty anthems we shall raise //

You have tested us and tried us / As silver is purified / In the net of great affliction, / Over our heads men did ride //

We went through the fire and water / But You brought us out, redeemed / You gave us a place of plenty / I will bring my offerings //

Promises I made to You, Lord / When I was in trouble deep / I will offer sacrifices / Incense, bullocks, goats and sheep //

Pause to think what God can do //

Come and listen, all who fear God / I will speak what He has done / My mouth and my soul cried to Him / And His Praise was on my tongue //

If I hold iniquity near, / My prayer the Lord will not hear / But I know that God has heard me / He attended to my needs //

Blessing be unto the Lord God / Who never turned back my prayer / Nor did He turn His Grace away / But His Mercy met me there

CHAPTER 67
"Let All the People Praise You"

God, be merciful and gracious / Unto us, and also bless us / May He make His face shine on us / Think on all the Lord does for us / That Your way be known on the earth / Your Salvation to all nations //
Let the people praise You, O God / Lord, let all the people praise You / Let the nations sing for gladness / You judge all people righteously / You lead all the nations on Earth / You govern continually //
Think on all the Lord does for us / Let the people praise You, Oh God / Lord, let all the people praise You / Then shall the earth yield its harvest / God, even our God shall bless us / Then all the nations of the Earth / Shall fear the Lord God Almighty

CHAPTER 68
"The God of Our Salvation"

Let God arise, let His enemies be scattered / Let all them that hate Him flee away from His Face / Drive them away just as smoke is driven away / As burning wax, let them melt in His Holy Place //
But let the righteous be joyful in God's Presence / Let them be glad and joyful in celebrations / Sing before God a song of praise unto His Name / By His Name JAH He rides the clouds in all nations //
Extol the Lord always, and rejoice before Him / Father to orphans and Husband to widows is / God who reigns on high in His Holy Dwelling Place / God sets the lonely in houses where no house is //
Families where there were no families before / He breaks the fetters and brings out the captives, free / He takes the rebels to desert captivity / Before His People He marched through the wilderness //
Meditate on all the things that the Lord has done / The earth quaked and the clouds poured rain before the Lord / Mount Sinai trembled at the God of Israel / You sent rain to refresh Your weary People, Lord //
Your Congregation lives by Your Confirmation / You have prepared good things for the poor and needy / The Lord gave the Word so that it could all be heard / The company that told it was a great army //

Kings and armies that fought the Lord did flee, did flee / The women on the Lord's side shared the spoils of war / Even those who stay to clean the animal stalls / Shall be prized as a silver dove with golden bars //

When Almighty God scatters the kings against Him / The ground of Salmon is white as new-fallen snow / The Hill of God is like the hill of Mount Bashan / A high Hill like Bashan, where few would dare to go //

Why have envy against the place God wants to live? / The holy hill of Zion is where God shall live / The Hill of God is where He lives forevermore / Yes, the Lord shall live in Mount Zion forever //

The Lord has twenty thousand chariots to ride / And thousands of angels to be close by His Side / The Lord is among them in the Holy Place, High / Just as He was when He gave the law on Sinai //

After You ascended into Heaven's Throne Room / You went to Hell to captivate the captives there / You gave gifts to all mankind, even to rebels / That the Spirit of the Lord could freely live there //

Blessed be the Lord God of the heavens and earth / Who loads us down with all benefits, one by one / He is God overall, Lord of our salvation / Meditate on all the things that the Lord has done //

He who is our God is God of all salvation / Unto the Lord God are issues of life and death / But God shall wound the head of all His enemies / And the hairy scalps of all who sin unto death //

The Lord said, I bring again rebels from Bashan / I will fetch them even from the depths of the sea / So your foot may be red from your enemies' blood / And your dogs' tongues dipped in blood from your enemies //

They have seen processions from Your Sanctuary / Oh God, my God, my King, in Your Sanctuary / First the singers, then the players of instruments / And the women in the middle with tambourines //

Bless God in the congregations, even the Lord, / All you that are of the fountain of Israel / Little Benjamin at the head with their rulers / Judah's princes and council, Zebulon's princes //

The princes of Naphtali, all strengthened by God / Strengthen, Oh God, that which You have worked to give us / To Your Temple at Jerusalem kings bring gifts / Stop the spearmen, bulls and calves that are against us //

Among their people of war every man shall give / They shall submit themselves with pieces of silver / All of the people who delight in making war / Shall be scattered until they study war no more //

Princes of God shall soon come out of Egypt's land / Ethiopia shall soon stretch her hands to God / Kingdoms of the Earth sing praises unto the Lord / Meditate on all the things that the Lord has done //

To God who rides upon the clouds which were of old / He thunders out His Voice, and that a Mighty Voice / Acknowledge the Strength that belongs to God alone / He rules over Israel by majestic choice //

Oh God, You are awesome from Your Holy Places / You are the God of Israel who gives more strength / You are the God who gives power to Your people / Blessed be the God of our salvation forever

CHAPTER 69
"The Truth of Your Salvation"

Save me, Oh God, for deep waters threaten my life / I sink in the deep miry clay, and cannot stand / I come into depth of waters overflowing //

When I cry, my eyes dry up because of crying / My throat is parched and dry, my eyes fail while I wait / While I wait for God, the haters keep on hating //

Haters causeless outnumber the hairs on my head / Enemy destroyers abound; but I restored / That which I never stole or destroyed anytime //

Lord, You know how guilty I have been and my sins / Are open to You, so do not let others slip, / Oh God, do not let Israel feel guilt or shame //

I have felt the sting of reproach for Your Name's Sake / I have become a stranger to my family / My brothers and sisters do not seem to know me //

Because the Zeal of Your House has eaten me up / And the reproaches that fell on You fell on me / I was reproached, even when I wept with fasting //

I clothed myself with sackcloth of humility / Thus I became a proverb of failure to them / Town leaders opposed me, drunkards sang about me //

But I will pray my prayer to You in such a way / That You in the multitude of Your Great Mercies / Hear me, and show me the Truth of Your Salvation //

Deliver me from the miry clay, let me rise / Let me be delivered from those with hateful eyes / Keep me from the floodwaters of deep affliction //

Do not let me be defeated from the water / Neither let the deep floodwaters pull me under / And do not let the pit shut its mouth upon me //

Hear my petition, Oh Lord, for You are loving / Hear me, for You are kind and good, and turn to me / Because You are filled with multitudes of mercies //

In Your Tenderness, do not hide Your Face from me / I am in trouble, please make haste to hear me now / I ask You right now to come near unto my soul //

I need Your Redeeming Power and Steadfast Love / Ransom me, deliver me from my enemies / You know the sin that brought on my reproach and shame //

You know the dishonor I brought on my own name / You know all the insults, the disgrace and the pain / You know all of my adversaries by their names //

I am brokenhearted because of my reproach / I am burdened down with a spirit of heaviness / I searched for compassion and comfort, but found none //

They poisoned my meat, gave me vinegar to drink / Let their table make them sick, and curse their blessings / Cause them to go blind, and set their loins to shaking //

Send out Your Fury toward them with Wrath and Anger / In palaces or tents, bring them desolation / Who persecute those already in affliction //

Who add pain and grief to those already wounded / Take their iniquity and add to it double / Instead of righteousness, Lord, send them more trouble //

Blot their names out of Your Eternal Book of Life / And do not let them be written with the righteous / But I am poor and needy, seeking to do right //

I sorrow after Your Salvation from on High / I will praise the Name of the Lord in joyful song / Lift Him up with thanksgiving who makes the weak strong //

This will please the Lord more than a burnt sacrifice / The afflicted, humble soul will see and rejoice / And the hearts of those shall live who make God their choice //

The Lord hears the prayer of the poor, helpless captive / Heaven, Earth, Seas, and whatever moves in these, praise Him / God will save Zion and Judah for possession //

Of cities for the children of all His Servants, / A place of inheritance for children's children / And they that love the Name of God shall dwell therein

CHAPTER 70
"My Help and My Deliverer"

Please hurry to deliver me / Oh Lord, please make haste to help me / Let those who hate me be ashamed / Whose mission is to destroy me //

Please send confusion to their minds / And let them be turned back in time / To nullify their evil plans / To hurt this poor and needy man //

When they go forward, send them back / Who jeer and say, Aha, Aha / Reward their shame, but let all those / Who seek Your Name rejoice in You //

With gladness let them magnify / Your Love, Salvation and Your Truth / But I am poor and needy, Lord, / Please hasten close to meet my need / My Help and my Deliverer / Please tarry not my soul to feed

CHAPTER 71
"The Strength of God Almighty"

Oh Lord, I place my trust in You / Give me a clear mind, not confused / Oh save me in Your Righteousness / Bring me to Your Deliverance //

Incline Your Ear unto my prayer / And save me when I meet You there / Be my rock of habitation / My hiding place in all nations //

You commanded angels to save / My rock and fortress from the grave / Deliver me from wicked men / From unrighteous and cruel hands //

Eternal hope You are to me / My trust from childhood is in Thee / You held me from my mother's womb / Forevermore I will praise You //

You show many wonders through me / But it is Your Refuge I seek / Let my mouth declare Your Praise and / Show Your Honor all the day //

Cast me not off in my old age / When my strength fails, do not forsake / My enemies speak against me / They take counsel to destroy me //

They say, God has left him alone / Take him down, for he is not strong / Persecute him, he has no one / To deliver him, so take him //

Oh God, be Thou not far from me / Oh my God, I call out to Thee / Send consternation, confusion / And consumption to all my foes //

My soul they would love to encroach / Cover them with their own reproach / Dishonor and shame is their fame / But I evermore seek Your Name //

In hope, and praise You more and more / Your Great Salvation I adore / Your Righteousness is new each day / The number is too great to say //

The Strength of God is where I go / Your Righteousness is all I know / Oh Lord, You taught me from my youth / And I have told Your Grace and Truth //

Now when I become old and gray / Forsake me not, Oh Lord, I pray / Let me show what Your Strength can do / This generation needs some proof //

And everyone that is to come / Needs righteousness, Most Holy One / Oh God, You are so very High / There is none like You, Adonai //

You have brought me through much trouble / Quicken me, Lord, on the double / And bring me up out of the depths / Increase my greatness with each step //

Comfort me so I can praise You / With psaltery and harp raise You / Oh Holy One of Israel / My lips rejoice, Your Truth I tell //

I sing to You, my soul redeemed / My tongue proclaims Your Righteous Deeds / My enemies are brought to shame / Confounded by Your Powerful Name //

The hurt they thought to bring to pass / Is over by Your Hand at last / The hurt is gone through Your Great Name / Your Love I evermore proclaim

CHAPTER 72

"Let The Whole Earth Be Filled With His Glory"

Oh Lord God, let the king have right judgments / Let Your Righteousness enter the king's son / He will judge your People with righteousness / He will judge the poor with Godly Judgment / Peace rules the mountains by Your Righteousness / And the little hills by Your Holiness //

He shall judge the poor and needy people / And save the children from hands of evil / They shall be filled, Oh Lord, with Godly Fear / For as long as the Sun and Moon endure / He shall come down with purity like rain / Showering down Truth and Grace by His Name //

The righteous shall flourish by His Right Hand / Peace shall abound so long as the Moon stands / He shall have dominion from Sea to Sea / From the River to the ends of the Earth / The wilderness dwellers shall bow to Him / His enemies shall lick His Dust in dearth //

Tarshish and the isles, Sheba and Seva / Shall offer gifts from lands, seas, rivers / All kings of the Earth shall bow before Him / All people from all nations shall serve Him / He shall deliver the needy who cry / Poor, helpless souls find in Him an ally //

He shall spare the poor and needy people / And save the souls of the needy people / From deceit and violence He shall redeem / Their blood, precious in the sight of their King / The gold of Sheba shall be given Him / Continual prayer shall be made for Him //

Daily He shall be praised and will prosper / Fruitful flourishing, on land and water / From mountaintops to cities on the plain / The Sun, Moon and Stars shall all praise His Name / All shall be blessed in the knowledge of Him / All nations shall call Him Blessed and bless Him //

Blessed be Adonai, God of Israel / He does wondrous things, He does all things well / Blessed be His Glorious Name forever / Let the whole Earth be filled with His Glory / Amen, and Amen. The prayers of David, / The son of Jesse, are now at an end.

CHAPTER 73
"Into the Sanctuary"

God is good to Israel / To those who are clean in heart / As for me, I was 'most gone / I almost had fallen far //

I was envious of fools / Evil men, yet prosperous / Painless are their souls in death / And in life, most vigorous //

They are not in trouble grim / Neither plagued like other men / Pride surrounds them like a chain / Violence robes them so vain //

If you peer into their eyes / They have more than one could prize / Fully wicked, they oppress / With corrupted loftiness //

They set evil plans to work / And their tongue walks through the earth / So God's Sons and His Daughters / Drink cups of bitter water //

And they ask, How does God know? / Does He know? and will He go? / Ungodly men prosper here / They increase in wealth held dear //

Have I cleansed my heart in vain? / And washed my hands for no gain? / All day long I have been plagued / Chastened with each passing day //

If I chose to speak like them / I would offend God's Children / When I looked around to see / It caused too much pain in me //

Into the Sanctuary, / Finally, I saw clearly / They walk a slippery slope / Destruction is in their scope //

They are in desolation / Fear without consolation / Terrified, as in a dream / Image tarnished and unclean //

With my attitude thus strained / I was stung with bitter pain / I was foolish and unlearned / Like a brute beast I did churn //

I continue still with You / Your Right Hand has pulled me through / You shall guide me with Your Eye / Then receive my soul on high //

Whom have I in Heaven but You? / On Earth, no one else will do / My flesh and my heart fail me / But God makes me strong and free //

He will all my portion be / For all of eternity / They shall die who stray from You / Those who serve false gods are through //

It is good to seek Your Face / I have trusted in Your Grace / I have placed my trust in You / Told the wondrous works You do

CHAPTER 74
"Why Have You Cast Us Off?"

Why have You cast us off forever? / Why assail the sheep of Your Pasture? / Remember Your congregation, God / Purchased of old, inheritance rod //

Which You redeemed, and where You have lived / See the destruction, unlivable / Evil roars in Your Congregation / Sets a banner against Your Nation //

It seemed like a thicket of trees there / Which lumberjacks hacked with their axes / Their men were famous for chopping trees / But now they smash carved work with ease //

They have burned Your Sanctuary down / Cast down Your Dwelling Place to the ground / They said in their hearts, destroy them all / Burned all God's Synagogues, small or tall //

We have no more signs, no more prophets / We have none with us that knows how long / Oh God, how long shall evil reproach? / Shall the enemy speak forever? //

Why do you withdraw Your Mighty Hand? / Pluck it out of Your Bosom again / For God is my King of Matchless Worth / Working Salvation in the whole Earth //

You broke the Sea with Your Mighty Hand / You crushed the whales' heads in Your Great Plan / You cut sea monsters' heads in pieces / Desert people ate in due seasons //

You stopped the fountains and the floodplain / Dried mighty rivers time and again / The Day is Yours, the Night is Yours, too / You have prepared the Sun and the Moon //

You set the borders of the whole Earth / Summertime, wintertime, harvest, dearth / The enemy has reproached You, Lord / Fools blasphemed Your Name with one accord //

Deliver not Your poor, needy son / To the multitude of wicked ones / Do not forget Your Congregation / The poor forever in all nations //

Let not the oppressed return ashamed / Let the poor and needy praise Your Name / Arise, Oh God, and plead Your Own Cause / Fools curse You daily, and break Your Laws / Remember what Your enemies say / Their tumult rises every day

CHAPTER 75
"Promotion Comes from God"

We give thanks to You, Oh God / We give thanks to You / For Your Name is near, Oh God, / Wondrous works You do //
In Your Congregation, Lord / I will judge in truth / All the Earth and People, Lord / Dissolve before You //
I bear the pillars of life / Says the Lord of life / Meditate on all His Works / All His Wondrous Works //
I said to the fools, Act not / In your foolishness / And to the wicked souls, / Leave off wickedness //
Do not be stiff-necked, Oh Man, / East, West, North or South, / For promotion comes from God, / It is in His Mouth //
One comes down and one comes up / By the Lord's Command / In the Cup the Wine is red / He mixes it by hand //
He pours Life out for all men / But the wicked souls / Take the wickedness within, / Drink without control //
I will sing forever true / Praise to Jacob's God / Wicked souls will I cut off / Righteous souls exalt

CHAPTER 76
"When God Arose"

In Judah is the Lord well-known / In Israel, His Name is Great / His Tabernacle in Salem / And His Dwelling-Place in Zion / Give silent witness to His Throne / Bow, Arrows, Shield and Sword gone //
Meditate upon His Power / More glorious than mountaintops / More excellent than prey that hops / The stout-hearted warriors / Are defeated by His Plans / They sleep the sleep of the dead //
No mighty men raised their hands, / God of Jacob, at Your Rebuke / The horse and chariot do rest / You alone are to be feared / No man can

stand in God's sight / When angered, all revere //
You gave judgment from Heaven / The Earth knew its place, and stayed / When God arose to judgment / To save all the meek that prayed / Meditate upon His Power / Even man's wrath turns to praise //
Whatever remains of wrath / You will redirect and raise / Give God what you have promised / Let all bring their precious things / He curbs the power of princes / He is awesome to all kings

CHAPTER 77
"My Song in the Night"

I cried unto the Lord with my voice / Even unto the Lord with my voice / And when I cried, the Lord heard my plea //
In my day of trouble I sought God / My tears flowed all night, and they ceased not / No comfort could my soul give to me //
I prayed to God when my trouble came / My spirit overwhelmed, I complained / Think upon the wonders of His Deeds //
You keep me far from all forms of rest / I am speechless in all my distress / Yet I think about the days of old //
When I think about the ancient times / I remember my song in the night / I speak to my heart, search my spirit //
Will the Lord cast us off forever? / Will He show favor to us never? / Is His Mercy gone forevermore? //
Is His Promise ever to fail us? / Has God forgotten to be gracious? / In anger closed His Tender Mercies? //
Think upon the wonders of His Deeds / I said, This is my infirmity / But I will remember all Your Deeds //
And the years of the Right Hand of God / I will remember the Most High God / The works and wonders of days of old //
Meditate and talk of Your Great Works / Your way is in Your House, Oh Lord God / None is so great a god as our God //
You are the God of Matchless Wonders / You show Your Strength, the people ponder / Israel's sons have ceased to wander //
Think upon the wonders of His Deeds / The waters saw You, Almighty God / The waters saw You, and were afraid //

The depths poured forth troublesome waters / The clouds poured out great thundershowers / The skies hurled thunder with great power //
Your Arrows of Lightnings launched abroad / Your Thunderclouds were heard in Heaven / With Your Lightnings, much light was given //
With power the Earth trembled and shook / Your Way is made known in the waters / Your Path made known in the great waters //
And the paths of Your Feet are unknown / You led Your People out like a flock / By Your Word they would go and then stop //
By the hand of Moses and Aaron / You led Your People out like a flock / By the hand of Moses and Aaron

CHAPTER 78
"A Table in the Wilderness"

Give ear, Oh people, to My Law / Incline your ears unto My Word / My Mouth shall speak in parables / Dark sayings we long ago heard //
Which our fathers taught us before / We will teach them to our children / Showing future generations / The praises and strength of God's wisdom //
And His Wonders to all nations / For He gave His Testimony / Israel's law to Moses given / He told our fathers to tell them //
To make them known to their children / That all generations would know / Even the children yet unborn / Who would tell them to their children //
That they would set their hope in God / And not forget His Wondrous Works / But keep all His Commandments true / Not as their fathers, who did shirk //
The stubborn and rebellious ones / Their generation was not right / Their spirit was not true to God / Young Ephraim so full of might //
A mighty army, bows and swords / Turned back in the day of warfare / Failed the Covenant of the Lord / Their hearts refusing His Law there //
Marvelous things did the Lord in / Egypt's land, the field of Zoan / He parted the seas, and then He / Marched them through the midst on dry land //

He led them daily with a cloud / And nightly with a fiery flame / He split rock in the wilderness / Out of the depths the waters came //

Streams of water flowed through the rock / Rivers flowed through the desert sands / And yet they sinned more against God / Provoking Him to show His Hand //

They tempted God in their dark hearts / Not manna, meat did they request / Not believing the Lord could set / A table in the wilderness //

He struck the rock, and the waters came / In the desert, streams overflowed / Can He give bread and flesh for us? / God heard this, and His Anger showed //

He sent a fire against Jacob / And anger against Israel / His Salvation had been so great / Yet they believed not in Him still //

Though He commanded clouds above / To open the doors of Heaven / And rained down Heavenly manna / The meat of angels was given //

Even though they ate angels' food / They all ate manna from Heaven / The East Wind and the South blew in / For their request, quail was given //

Feathered fowls like sands of the sea / All around their tents were fallen / They ate until they ate their fill / For He allowed their lust chosen //

They were not strangers to their lust / But while their meat was in their mouths / God turned their strongest men to dust / The warriors of Israel's house //

For all this they believed Him not / Through all the works that He had done / They spent their days in vanity / In trouble their lives were undone //

When some of them died, they returned / They sought Him early, and inquired / They remembered that God was their Rock / Sought what their Redeemer required //

Yet they flattered Him with their mouths / And lied unto Him with their tongues / For their heart was not right with Him / His Covenant was not their home //

Compassionately, He forgave / Their many sins, destroyed them not / He turned His Anger much away / His Wrath He would not stir too hot //

For He remembered they were dust / A wind that passes not again / They mocked Him in the wilderness / Provoked Him in the desert sands //

They turned back and then tempted God / And limited the Holy One / Of Israel, forgot His Hand / How He delivered all along //

From His Miracles in Egypt / To His Wonders in Zoan's field / He turned their waters into blood / They could not drink, it was revealed //

He sent all sorts of flies to them / Devouring them, and frogs, too / To destroy them, and their increase / Was meat for the caterpillar, //

And their labor for the locust / Their vines He destroyed with hail / Their sycamores with icy hail / He gave their cattle to the hail //

And their flocks to lightning flashes / He sent them His Fierce, Hot Anger / His Indignant Wrath and Trouble, / He sent angels on the double //

He helped His Anger to get in / Spared not their soul from death for sin / Gave their life to the pestilence / Smote all Egyptian firstborn men //

The tabernacles of Ham shook / With the loss of their rightful heirs / But His People He led like sheep / He led them in wilderness deep //

He led them safely with no fear / The sea swallowed their enemies / He brought them to Mount Sinai / Bordering His Sanctuary //

He purchased it with His Right Hand / Cast out the heathen in the land / Divided their inheritance / The tribes of Israel in tents //

Yet they tempted and provoked God / Kept not the Lord's Testimonies / They turned back unfaithfully / Turned aside deceitfully //

They provoked Him from high places / Jealousy from idolatry / When God heard this, He was angry / He abhorred Israel fully //

He forsook His Tabernacle, / Shiloh's tent He placed among men / His Strength went to captivity / His Glory to the enemy //

He gave His People to the sword, / Angry with His Inheritance, / Fire consumed their young men and their / Maidens had no one to marry //

Their priests fell by the sword's power / And their widows had not lamented / God rose up as though out of sleep / A strong man from wine fermented //

He struck His enemies' rear flanks / Put them in continued retreat / The tabernacle of Joseph, / Ephraim's tribe, He gave no seat //

But chose the tribe of Judah fair / And Mount Zion, His High Palace, / Like the Earth, forever given, / His Sanctuary unto Heaven //

He chose David for a servant / Took him from leading his small flock / From following ewes great with young / He brought him to feed His People //

Jacob the sheep of His Pasture / And Israel His Inheritance / He fed them with integrity / And guided them with skillful hands

CHAPTER 79

"For the Glory of Your Name"

Oh God, hordes of heathen have attacked / They have ransacked Your Inheritance / They have defiled Your Holy Temple / Turning Jerusalem to rubble //

They have given the dead bodies of / Your Servants to be meat for the birds / The corpses of Your Dead Saints to be / Feasts for the beasts of prey in the Earth //

The blood of Your People have they shed / As water around Jerusalem / In all the death and destruction shed / There was no one left to bury them //

Daily our neighbors do reproach us / They heap scorn and derision on us / How long, Lord, are You angry with us? / Will Your Jealous Fire burn eternal? //

Pour Your Anger out on these pagans / Who have never acknowledged You, Lord / And also upon all the nations / Who have never called upon Your Name //

For they have devoured Jacob, made / His dwelling place a desolation / Please remember not against us, Lord, / The sins of our fathers before us //

Let tender mercies come before us / Send Your Help, for we are very shamed / Help us, Oh God of our salvation / Help us for the glory of Your Name //

Deliver us, purge us from our sins / Oh Lord, we pray this for Your Name's Sake / Lest the heathen say, Where is their God? / Revenge the blood of Your Servants shed //

Hear the prisoners by Your Power / Greatly preserve those who would be dead / Render to our neighbors sevenfold / The reproach wherewith they have reproached //

It is You they have reproached, Oh Lord / But we will give You thanks forever / Your People, the sheep of Your Pasture / Shall praise Your Great Name forevermore

CHAPTER 80
"Visit This Vine"

Give ear, Oh Great Shepherd of Israel / Thou who lead'st Joseph like a flock of sheep / Thou that dwellest between the cherubims / Shine forth Thy Light and save us from the deep //

In front of Ephraim and Benjamin / In front of Manasseh stir up Thy Strength / Come and save us, turn us to Thee again / Cause Thy Face to shine on us, and heal us //

Oh Lord God of hosts, how long wilt Thou be / Against the prayer of Thy People, angry? / Thou feedest them with bread of tears to eat / And givest them water of tears to drink //

Thou makest us a strife to our neighbors / Our enemies mock and laugh over us / Turn us, and cause Thy Face to shine on us / We shall be saved by Thy Power in us //

Thou hast brought a vine from out of Egypt / Thou cast out the heathen, and planted it / Thou madest room before it, and caused it / To take deep root, and it filled all the land //

This vine covered the hills with its shadow / The boughs of this vine, like cedars hung low, / This vine sent out her boughs to the ocean / This vine's branches into the river flowed //

Why hast Thou broken down this vine's hedges? / All they which pass by the way pluck her dry / The boar of the wood doth stop to waste it / The wild beast of the field doth devour it //

Return, we beseech Thee, Oh God of Hosts / And on Thy Return, look down from Heaven / Return, and behold, and visit this vine / And the vineyard which Thy Hand hath given //

And the branch which Thou made strong for Thyself / It is burned and cut, the people perish / At the rebuke of Thy Countenance, gone / Let Thy Hand on the Son of Man be strong //

To the man whom Thou made strong for Thyself / And we will not turn from following Thee / Turn us once again, Oh Lord God of hosts / And we will not turn from following Thee //

Turn this vine again, Oh Lord God of Hosts / Turn us, and on us cause Thy Face to shine / Turn us once again, Oh Lord God of Hosts / Turn this vine again, and visit this vine

CHAPTER 81

"God Our Strength"

Sing a song to God our strength, / Make a joyful noise to the God of Jacob / Take a psalm with tambourine / Sing a song with the sweet lyre and psaltery //

Sound the shofar at new moon / The appointed time of the solemn feast day / For a law in Israel, / And a judgment of the God of Jacob //

For a strong testimony / Of the God who went through the land of Egypt / Said an unfamiliar voice / I removed the burden from his shoulder //

No more load of slavery / You called Me in trouble, I delivered Thee / In the place of thunder clouds / At the waters of Meribah, I proved Thee //

Think about what God has done / Meditate upon His Mercy and Judgment / Hear, My People, what I say / Israel, if you will hearken unto Me //

No strange god shall be in thee / Neither shalt thou worship any God but Me / For I am the Lord Thy God / And I brought thee out of the land of Egypt //

If you open your mouth wide / With the blessings of the Lord I will fill it / But My People would not hear, / And the land of Israel would not have me //

So I gave them to their lust, / And they walked in the counsel of their own minds / If My People had heard me, / Israel walking in the ways of the Lord, //

I had crushed their enemies, / Turned My Hand against all their adversaries / All the haters of the herd / Soon would have submitted themselves unto Him //

Their time forevermore / He had given them the best of His Storehouse / With sweet honey from the rock / I should have satisfied thee forevermore

CHAPTER 82

"God Stands in the Congregation"

God stands in the congregation / Of the judges of the Earth / How long will You judge unfairly, / Accepting wicked works? //

Meditate on the day of the Lord / Defend the poor and fatherless / Do kindness to the needy / Deliver the afflicted souls //

From wicked men and greedy / They neither know, nor understand, / In darkness they roam the land / The foundations of the whole Earth //

Are being moved out of course / In times past I said you are / Children of the Most High God / But you shall die as other men //

And fall like a prince in sin / Arise, Oh God, and judge the Earth / All the nations shall be Yours / They shall all bow down to You

CHAPTER 83

"Let Them Know You Are Lord of All"

Keep not Your Silence, Oh Lord God / Hold not Your Peace, and be not still / Oh God, Your enemies make war / They that hate You joined against Your Will //

They have taken counsel as one / Drafting plans against Your People / They have consulted to destroy / Israel from all the nations //

They have said, Let us cut them off / From ever being a nation / That the name of Israel might be / Forgotten among all people //

They have consulted and agreed / They have joined forces against Thee / Edomites and Ishmaelites / Moabites with the Hagarenes //

Gebal, Ammon, and Amalek / Citizens of Tyre, Philistines / Ashur has joined forces with them / The children of Lot are with them //

Meditate on what God can do / Make them as the Midianites / Who fought Your Servant Gideon / As Sisera, and Jabin were, //

Stopping at the brook of Kison / Men of war perished at Endor / They were as manure on the ground / Nobles joined like Oreb, and Zeeb //

Who died on their own property / Or as Zebah and Zalmunnah, / Who tried a vain conspiracy / Tried to overtake God's Property //

Make them, Lord, as wheels in the dust / As the stubble before the wind / As wood is consumed in the fire / As the flame sets mountains on fire //

Terrify them in Your Tempest / And make them afraid in Your Storm / Let their faces be filled with shame, / Oh Lord, that they may seek Your Name //

Let them be confused and troubled / Let them be ashamed, and perish / Who do not call on Your Great Name / That all may know God is the Lord //

Let them know You are Lord of all

CHAPTER 84

"Even the Sparrow Has Found Her Place"

How lovely are Your Dwelling Places / Oh Lord God of hosts / My soul desires and even faints for / The Courts of the Lord //

My heart and my flesh are crying out / For the living God / Even the sparrow has found a place, / The swallow a nest //

A place where she may lay her young / Your Altars, Oh Lord / Oh Lord God of Hosts, my God and King / Blessed are those who dwell in Your House //

Always praising You / Meditate on what the Lord can do / Blessed is the man whose strength is in You / Whose heart knows Your Ways //

Passing through the dry Bakaa Valley / They make it a well / Springs of crystal clear water with rain / Filling up the pools //

From strength to strength they go before God / They all appear there / Please hear my plea, Oh Lord God of Hosts / To my prayer give ear //

Meditate on what the Lord can do / Behold the face of Your Anointed / Oh Lord God, our Shield / Far better is one day in Your Courts //

Than thousands elsewhere / I would linger at the threshold of the House of the Lord / Rather than dwell with wicked men in wicked tents / The Lord God is our Defense and Light //

With Grace and Glory / He will not keep back any good thing / To those who walk right / Oh Lord of Hosts, blessed are all those who // Put their trust in You

CHAPTER 85
"I Will Hear What the Lord Has To Say"

Lord, You have shown favor to Your Land / You brought Jacob from captivity / You have covered the price for their sin / You forgave all their iniquity //

Meditate upon His Mighty Deeds / You have taken away all anger / You have turned away from fierce anger / Turn us to You, God of Salvation //

Cause Your Anger toward us to cease / Will You be angry with this nation? / Store anger for all generations? / Lord, will You not revive us again, //

So the people may rejoice in You? / Show us Your Mercy, Oh Lord of Hosts, / And give us eternal salvation / I will hear what the Lord has to say //

He will speak peace unto His People / He will bring peace unto all His Saints / But they must covenant to obey / Determine never to turn away //

His salvation guides them that fear Him, / The Glory of God dwelling in them / Mercy and truth have made a meeting / Righteousness and peace exchanged greetings //

Truth shall spring out of the rich, deep earth / Righteousness shall rejoice from Heaven / The Lord shall give good to His People / And our land shall give good increase //

Righteousness shall go before the Lord / And He shall lead us in His Pathways

CHAPTER 86
"Wholehearted Praise"

Bow down thine ear, Oh Lord / Hear me, for I am needy / Keep my poor, needy soul / Unto You I am holy //

Save Thy Servant, Oh Lord / That daily trusteth in Thee / Show mercy to me, Lord / I cry out to Thee daily //
Joy of my soul restore / For I lift my soul to Thee / Thou art good, forgiving, / Merciful to those who call //
To all who call on Thee / Give ear to my prayer, Lord / Look to my supplications / In trouble I will call //
In all nations You will answer / No god is like You, Lord / No works are like unto Yours / All nations worship You //
All shall glorify Your Name / You are great and wondrous / None is like You, Lord of all / Teach me Your Way, Oh Lord //
I will walk in truth always / Give my heart Your Power / I will always fear Your Name / Wholehearted praise I give //
I will glorify Your Name / Your Mercy exceeds all / Forever it is for me / You delivered my soul //
From the grave that had called me / Proud men rise against me / Violent men have sought me / They have not called on Thee //
You are Compassionate, and / You are Gracious, and You are / Merciful and Patient / You are the Giver of Truth //
Turn to me with mercy / Lord give Your Strength unto me / The son of Your Handmaid / Give me a Godly Signal //
Let them who hate me see, / And be ashamed, for You, Lord / Helped and comforted me

CHAPTER 87
"The Lord's Countdown"

God has a Holy Countdown / Souls born in the Holy Mountain //
God loves the Gates of Zion / More than Jacob's earthly dwelling //
The countdown of souls is great / Glorious things, glorious place //
God's Eternal City of rest / Meditate on God's Salvation. //
I will mention Rahab there / Once a harlot, now a queen //
Some from Babylon are there / Once served mammon, now serve the King //
Some from Philistia there / Who used to take, now give freely //
Tyre and Ethiopia / Proud people find humility //
Impossible it may seem / But many souls were saved from there //
Of Zion it shall be said / This soul and that were born in her, //

And the Lord God Almighty / Shall comfort and establish her //
When cometh the Lord's Countdown / When He enrolls the people there //
In Zion, it shall be found, / The places where souls were born there //
Meditate on God's Salvation / The singers sing God's Praises //
The players of instruments play / All the appointed people //
Shall give their praises unto Thee / All the springs of refreshing //
Are in Thee, City of the King

CHAPTER 88

"*I Have Stretched Out My Hands To You*"

Oh Lord God of my salvation / Before You day and night I cry / Let my prayer arise before You / Listen as I cry and sigh //
My mortal soul full of trouble / Is drawing near unto the grave / The slimy pit of Hell would take me / My soul alone lacks strength to save //
My life cannot be appointed / To tell Your Works or do Your Will / In death no longer remembered / Cut off from Mercy's Hand, and still //
I have been in deep depression / Darkness has overwhelmed my soul / Separated from Your Presence / Affliction would swallow me whole //
Think on God's Mercy and Judgment //
A faithful friend is hard to find / My soul is cast away from them / Shut up in abomination / I cannot come forth to seek them //
Affliction makes my eyes to cry / Unto the Lord both day and night / Lord, I have daily called on You / I have stretched out my hands to You //
Shall the dead receive Your Wonders / Or arise to give You Honors? / Wherein shall the dead spread Your Fame / Or sing the Praises of Your Name //
Think on God's Mercy and Judgment //
Shall Your Lovingkindness be known / In the grave, or Faithfulness shown? / In the dark, where is righteousness? / Declared in death's forgetfulness? //

Unto You, Oh Lord, have I cried / Rivers of tears both day and night / I have stretched out my hands to You / Early in the morning to You //

Lord, why would You cast off my soul? / Why would You hide Your Face from me? / From my youth I am afflicted / In terror I am distracted //

Wrath and terrors do surround me / Like waters daily around me / Together they have compassed me / Separated from all but You //

Who could love me in this my plight? / Befriend me in this my station? / Acquaint himself with my dark grief? / You alone, God of my salvation

CHAPTER 89

"Your Mercy Covenant"

I will ever sing the Lord's Mercies / I will speak Your Faithfulness to all / Heaven and Earth build up Your Mercy / From the heavens, Your Faithfulness falls //

The Lord has said, My Covenant is / With David My Chosen, My Servant / Your seed I establish forever / Build your throne to all generations //

Meditate on what the Lord can do //

The heavens declare Your Wondrous Works / Lord, the saints declare Your Faithfulness / Who in Heaven can compare to You? / Who on Earth can do what You can do? //

Fear the Lord in the congregation / Revere Him in every nation / God of Hosts, who is as strong as You? / Who spreads faithfulness around like You? //

You control the sea, lest it should rage / When the storms rise, You calm the dark waves / You have broken Egypt's slavery / As a strong man smitten before Thee //

You have scattered all Your enemies / Your Strong Arm has brought the victory / The heavens are Yours, the Earth is Yours / The world and all the fullness therein //

The North is Yours, and the South is Yours / The treasures thereof, You founded them / Mount Tabor and Mount Hermon rejoice / When You thunder with Your Mighty Voice //

Your Arm is Mighty, Your Name Holy / Your Hand is Strong, Your Right Hand is High / Justice and judgment live at Your Throne / Mercy and truth see Your Face alone //

The people who know the sound of joy / Shall walk, Lord, in Your Marvelous Light / Your Countenance shall light all their way / In Your Name they shall rejoice all day //

In Your Righteousness shall they be raised / You are their glory and their strong praise / Your favor is the exaltation / Of Israel, Your Holy Nation //

The Lord God is our Defense, and the / Holy One of Israel our King / You spoke to Samuel in the night, / And said, I have helped a man of might //

I have found David My Chosen One / My Servant and My Anointed One / With My Oil have I anointed him / With My Hand have I appointed him //

With My Holy Arm shall strengthen him / None shall defeat or overcome him / I shall beat his foes before his face, / And those who hate him will I disgrace //

I will prosper his hand in the sea, / And his power in all the rivers / He shall cry Abba, Father to me / My Rock, My Salvation, My Father //

I will make him as My Firstborn Son / Higher than the Kings of all the Earth / Keep My Mercy with him evermore / As sun, moon, stars, sands on the seashore //

His seed shall endure forevermore / His kingdom as the days of Heaven / If his children leave My Law, desert / My Judgments, break My Statutes, stray from //

My Commandments, I will visit them / Punishing their disobedience, / And their guilty souls will know My Pain / But My Covenant, made in My Name //

My Covenant of Lovingkindness / I will not utterly take from him / Neither shall My Faithfulness fail him / For this is My Covenant with him //

I will not change what I have promised / Once by My Holiness I did speak / My Unfailing Promise to David / His seed shall endure eternally //

His throne shall be as the morning sun / Established forever as the moon / As a faithful witness in Heaven / Meditate on what the Lord can do //

But You have rejected Your Chosen / Been angry with Your Anointed One / You annulled Your Holy Covenant / You cast down the Crown of Your Chosen //

His hedges are broken down to see / His strongholds are in ruination / He is plundered by those who pass by / His neighbors reproach his condition //

The strength of his adversaries grows / You have made his enemies quite glad / You have turned the power of his sword / And caused his battle plans to go bad //

His glory has become his disdain / His throne is on the ground with his name / His youthful days You have pushed aside, / And You have covered the king with shame //

Meditate on what the Lord can do / How long, Lord, before we can see You? / Will Your Wrath like fire forever burn? / Remember how short my time to turn //

To what end are all men made in vain? / What man lives who shall not see death, too? / Shall he escape his soul from the grave? / Meditate on what the Lord can do //

Where are Your past Lovingkindnesses? / Which You swore unto David in truth? / Remember the shame of Your Servants / I have borne their reproach since my youth //

The reproach of all Your Mighty Ones / To whom Your enemies have reproached / Oh Lord, Your enemies have reproached / The footsteps of Your Anointed One //

The footsteps of Your Servant David / Shall yet find Your Mercy Covenant / Blessed be the Lord God forevermore / Amen, and Amen

CHAPTER 90

"Our Dwelling Place"

Lord, You have been our dwelling place / For all time it has been this way / Before the first mountain was made / Before the Earth formed from void space / Between the two eternities / You are God //

You say when man shall meet his end / Yet say, Return, children of men / A thousand years in Your Sight is / As yesterday or yesternight / You carry them as with a flood / As nightfall, as morning grass / Which springs up //

The morning grass springs up at dawn / By eventide it is cut back / Even so are Your Children, Lord, / Consumed by anger, trouble, wrath / You have set our sins before You / Our secret sins are brought to light / Our lives like a tale that is told / In Your Wrath //

Our days are threescore years and ten, / And if by strength they be fourscore / Yet there is labor and sorrow / Soon cut off, and we know no more / Who knows the strength of Your Anger? / The fear of God abates anger / Teach us to number all our days / To apply our hearts to wisdom //

Return, Lord //

How long until You turn around / Your Servants lying on the ground? / Satisfy us with Your Mercy / We will rejoice, we will be glad / Make us as glad as we were sad / Make us good as we were evil / Show Your Work unto Your Servants, / And Your Glory to Your People / Beautify! //

Let Your Beauty be upon us / Establish Your Work within us / Yes, our handiwork establish, / Confirm it!

CHAPTER 91
"In the Secret Place"

He who lives in the secret place / Of the Most High shall live in grace / Under the Almighty's shadow //

I will say of the Lord, He is / My fortress, my God, hiding place / I will trust in Him forevermore //

He shall deliver You from the / Snare of the fowler, and from the / Plague of God's great calamities //

He will take you under His Wing / You shall learn trust under His Wing / His Truth shall be your spear and shield / You shall not fear nighttime terrors / You shall not fear daytime arrows / The night sickness / The daytime scourge //

If a thousand fall at your side / Ten thousand fall at your right hand / It shall never come near to you //

Only with your eyes beholding / The wicked reward unfolding / You will rejoice in the Lord God //

Because you have made the Lord God / Of my secret place of refuge / Even the most High dwelling-place, //

The place of your habitation / No evil shall take your station / No plague come near to where you live //

His angels have watch over you / They keep you in all that you do / Lest you should stumble in your walk //

You shall tread upon the lions / You shall tread upon the serpents / Young lions and serpents trample //

He has loved Me with his whole heart / Undeserving of any part / I will deliver him for this //

I will set him in a high place / In a fruitful, not a dry place / As he has daily called My Name //

He shall call, and I will answer / His trouble I will deliver / Deliver him and honor him //

I will bless him with a long life / Satisfy him throughout his life / And will show him my salvation

CHAPTER 92

"It Is A Good Thing"

It is a good thing to give thanks / Unto the Lord and praise Your Name / Oh Most High, You are loving, kind / In the morning, faithful at night //

Upon the harp of David play / And also on the psaltery / With solemn sound do meditate / Upon the goodness of the Lord //

Oh, Lord, Your Work has made me glad / Successful in works by Your Hands / Oh, Lord, how mighty are Your Works / Your thoughts are very deep to man //

The rough and violent know not / Neither does the foul understand / When the wicked as morning grass / Spring up, and evil men do stand //

Flourish they in evil? Never! / They shall be cut off forever / But You, Lord, are Almighty God / And all Your enemies shall die //

All evil workers shall be scattered / But You, Lord, shall enhance my strength / As the horn of a one-horned beast / With fresh oil shall You anoint me //

My eyes shall see enemies fall / My ears shall hear wicked plans fail / The righteous shall grow like the palm / Like the cedar in Lebanon //

Those who plant themselves in God's House / Flourish in the Courts of the Lord / They shall be fruitful when old / They shall be successful and bold //

They shall prove the Lord upright / Kind, loving, faithful day and night / The Lord is my rock, strong and sure / His Righteousness ever endures

CHAPTER 93
"The Lord Reigns"

The Lord reigns, He is majestic / Clothed with strength which He has put on //

And this world He has established / Cannot be moved, it is so strong //

Forever Your Throne is settled / As old as forever is long //

The mighty floods lift up their voice / Oh Lord, we hear the angry waves //

The Lord is stronger than the noise / Than the mightiest sea can raise //

Your Testimonies are all true / Your House is beautiful as You //

Because of Holiness Divine / It shall be standing for all time

CHAPTER 94
"Show Yourself, God"

Lord God, we know vengeance belongs to You / To You who owns vengeance, Show Yourself, God / The Judge of the Earth, we know it is You / Judge the proud evildoers, Oh Lord God //

Oh Lord God, about all the wicked souls / How long shall all the wicked souls prosper? / How long shall they utter their blasphemy? / How long shall they boast of iniquity? //

They break Your Children into pieces, Lord / They afflict Your Heritage with evil / Lord, they kill widows, strangers and orphans / They say, The Lord doesn't see the evil //

Understand this, you violent people, / And you foolish ones, when will you be wise? / He who made the ear, shall He not hear you? / He who formed the eye, shall He not see you? //

He who chastises all the heathen souls, / Shall He not correct you with affliction? / He who teaches knowledge to all mankind, / Shall He not know when you plan rebellion? //

The Lord knows the thoughts of every man / He knows all the vanity that they plan / Blessed is the man whom You chasten, Oh Lord / Blessed is he whom You teach out of Your Law //

You give him rest from adversity, Lord / Until the grave is digged for the outlaw / The Lord will not turn away His People / The Lord will not spurn His Inheritance //

God's judgment of evil brings righteousness / His Children will follow His Righteousness / Who will rise with me against the evil / Or stand with me against iniquity? //

Without God, I had suffered in silence / When I cried, the Lord had mercy on me / He held me up, lest my foot had fallen / As I ponder, You bring comfort to me //

Shall evil rulers fellowship with You / Those who frame lawlessness into a law? / They collide against souls of righteous men, / And condemn the blood of the innocents //

But my Lord is my tower of defense, / And my God is the anchor of my strength / He shall return all their iniquity / And cut them off in all their evil deeds //

Yes, the Lord God Almighty, it is He / Who shall judge all their wicked, evil deeds

CHAPTER 95
"Come Let Us Sing"

Come let us sing unto the Lord, / And make a joyful noise to Him / The Rock of our salvation, Come / Before His Presence with a song //

With joyful noise of thanksgiving / Let us bring unto Him our psalms / For God is a great God and King / He is King above everything //

His Hand reaches the deep places / The strong hills are His to command / The Sea is His, for He made it, / And His Hands formed all the dry land //

Come let us worship and bow down / Let us kneel before our maker / For the Lord God, He is our God / We are the sheep of His pasture //

We are His People, by His Hand / If you will hear His Voice today / Do not let your heart turn away / As in the provocation, and //

In the wilderness temptation / Your ancestors had unbelief / They tempted me and tested me / They saw my work, they gave me grief //

With forty years of unbelief / As they wandered in the desert / I knew the error of their heart / They refused My Ways, My Wisdom //

That I would to them impart / They provoked Me unto anger / A people that should have been blessed / If they had chosen My Ways, they // Would have entered into My Rest

CHAPTER 96

"Sing Unto the Lord A New Song"

Sing unto the Lord a new song / Sing unto the Lord, all the earth //
Sing unto the Lord, bless His Name / Show His Salvation day by day //
Tell His Glory to the heathen / Tell His Wonders to the people //
God is great, greatly to be praised / Above all gods of all people //
Among all gods of all nations / God alone made Earth and Heaven //
Give Him Honor and Majesty / Ascribe to Him Strength and Beauty //
In His Sanctuary give Him / Oh you kindreds of all give Him //
Give unto Him Glory and Strength / Give unto Him Glory due Him //
The Glory due unto His Name / Unto Him bring an offering //
Come into His Courts with worship / In the beauty of holiness //
Give Him Reverence, all the Earth / Tell the heathen He rules the Earth //

The world is firmly by God / It is strong and unmovable //
Righteous is the judge, the Lord God / He shall judge the people rightly //
Let the heavens rejoice, let the / Earth be glad and lift its voice, Let //
The Sea roar, its waves praise the Lord / Let the field be full of joy //
Let all that is within the field / Rejoice, and all the trees rejoice //
Before the Lord, He is coming / To judge the earth, He is coming //
He shall judge the people rightly / He shall judge them with His Truth

CHAPTER 97
"Zion Heard All About It"

The Lord reigns the Earth from His Throne on High / Let the Earth rejoice, the islands be glad / He rides the thick clouds in the darkest night / He rules with Righteousness, Justice and Light //

He sends consuming fire against His foes / His lightnings paint wherever He goes / The hills melt like wax at the Lord's Presence / The presence of the Lord of all the Earth //

The heavens declare the Lord's righteousness / The people see the Lord is glorious / He confuses all who worship idols / Graven images bow to worship Him //

Zion heard all about it, and was glad / Judah rejoiced in Your Judgments of them / Oh Lord, You are High above all the Earth / Above all who are called gods, but are not //

All you who love the Lord, hate all evil / God protects His Saints from every blot / He saves them from the hand of evil men / Sows light for their path and gladness for them //

Rejoice in the Lord, all who are righteous / Give thanks to remember His Holiness

CHAPTER 98
"All The Earth Has Seen His Salvation"

Sing unto the Lord a new song / For He has performed wonderful things //

His Power and His Hand of Truth / Have gotten for Him the victory //
The Lord has shown His Salvation / His Righteousness to all the Nations //
He has given Mercy and Truth / To all the nations, to Israel //
From the corners of the whole Earth / People know His Salvation is real //
Unto the Lord make joyful noise / Let all the Earth proclaim with loud noise //
Let all the Earth sing praise to Him / Sing to God with the sound of the harp //
With the voice of a psalm praise Him / Trumpets and cornets sound crisp and sharp //
Make a joyful noise unto Him / Make a joyful noise unto the King //
Let the Sea roar, and all in it / Let the world shout, all inhabitants //
Let all the floods show their whitecaps / Let all the hills rejoice together //
Before the Lord, for He cometh / The Lord cometh to judge the whole Earth //
With righteousness the Lord cometh / To judge all people with equity

CHAPTER 99

"Exalt the Lord God on High"

God reigns, the people tremble / He sits between the cherubims //
Let the whole Earth stagger before Him / The Lord is great in Zion //
He sits high above all people / Bring praise to His Great and Awesome Name //
The Name of God is holy / Our King reigns in Truth and Mercy //
You judge equitably in Jacob / Exalt the Lord God on high //
At His Footstool worship His Might / For He is Holy before all things //
Moses and Aaron the priests, / And Samuel with the prophets //
Are among them that called on His Name / They all called upon the Lord //

And He answered every one / Communing in the cloudy pillar //
They kept His Testimonies, / And all of His Ordinances //
Oh Lord our God, You did answer them / You brought them all forgiveness //
Destroyed their wicked intentions / You are worthy to be exalted //
Serve Him with exaltation / At the holy hill of Zion //
Our Lord God Almighty is holy

CHAPTER 100
"Make A Joyful Noise"

Make a joyful noise / To God, all the earth //
Serve Him and be glad / Sing with joyful mirth //
The Lord, He is God / He has made us all, //
And not we ourselves / We are His People //
He is our Shepherd / His Gates deserve thanks //
His Courts deserve praise / Be thankful to God //
His Holy Name raise / God is good, and His //
Mercy unfailing / His Truth extends to //
All generations

CHAPTER 101
"I Will Watch The Faithful Ones"

Of Mercy will I sing / Of Judgment will I sing / Unto You, Lord, will I sing //
I will conduct myself / Perfectly and wisely / Lord, when will You come to me? //
I keep a perfect heart / I keep wicked things out / I hate those who turn away //
No divided heart here / No evil men kept here / Slanderers shall be cut off //
I hate all haughtiness / I hate all pridefulness / I will watch the faithful ones //
Faithful ones will stay here / Perfect hearts will serve me / Liars shall not dwell with me //

Deceivers shall not stay / Those who lie shall not stay / I will destroy all evil //

Evil men have no place / Wicked men a disgrace / To the city of the Lord

CHAPTER 102
"He Hears the Prisoner's Cry"

Oh Lord, hear my prayer / Let my cry come to You / Hide not from me in trouble / Answer quickly when I call You //

My days are burned away like smoke / As bones on the hearth make smoke / My heart withered, broken / My bread uneaten //

Like a pelican / Like a lone desert owl / Like a sparrow on the roof / In my wilderness affliction //

All my enemies reproach me / All day long they reproach me / They covenant against me / Sackcloth and ashes //

Bread of affliction, tears / Mingled in all my drink / Your Wrath has spun me around / You lifted me up, cast me down //

My days are like a short shadow / Withered like grass in the meadow / Lord, You live forever / Always remembered //

Lord, You shall arise / With Mercy in Zion / It is her time of favor / The set time of favor is come //

Her precious stones are much treasured / Even her dust is favored / The Nations fear the Lord / Kings fear Thy Glory //

When God builds Zion / He shall come in glory / He will hear the poor man's prayer / Receive the prayer of the lonely //

For all time this shall be written / Unborn Nations shall praise God / From His Sanctuary / Earth was seen by God //

God beheld the Earth / From His Holy Heaven / He hears the prisoner's cry / Saves those to whom death was given //

To shout the power of His Name / In Zion, declare His Praise / Within Jerusalem / When people gather //

Kingdoms together / Come to serve the Lord God / My strength turned into weakness / My health was shortened in sickness //

I said, Lord, shorten not my days / Your Days exist forever / You laid Earth's foundation / The sky is Your Work //

They age, but not You / As a garment they age / You shall change them in Your Time / Then they shall be forever changed //

You never change, You are the same / Your Years have no end in sight / Your Seed shall continue / Powered by Your Might

CHAPTER 103

"*Bless the Lord, Oh My Soul*"

Bless the Lord, Oh my soul / Bless His Name with all strength / Bless the Lord, Oh my soul / His Benefits at length //
He forgives all your sin / Heals you when you are sick / Saves you from destruction / Gives good, kind instruction //
Fills your mouth with good things / Gives strength like an eagle / God is fair and righteous / To all who are oppressed //
Moses and Israel / Knew His Way, how He blessed / Merciful and gracious / Rarely angry with us //
Plenteous in Mercy / He will not always scold / He is not quick to judge / Nor give what we deserve //
His Mercy is as high / As Heaven is to Earth / To all who fear the Lord / As far as East from West //
He covers all our sins / As fathers do children / He knows that we are weak / He knows that we are dust //
He knows we are as grass / As flowers and as plants / The wind passes over / It is gone forever //
Its bloom shall be no more / But the Lord's Mercy is / Forever and ever / To all them that fear Him //
And their children's children / His Righteousness is true / To those who keep His Law / God's Throne is in Heaven //
His Kingdom rules us all / Bless the Lord, you angels / Excellent in Power / Doing His Commandments //
Listening each hour / Bless the Lord, all His Hosts / You ministers of His / Doing all His Pleasure //
Bless the Lord, all His Works / In all parts and places / Where He has dominion / The Lord rules over all //
Bless the Lord, Oh my soul

CHAPTER 104
"He Walks on the Wings of the Wind"

I will bless the Lord, Oh my soul / Oh Lord my God, how great You are //
Honor and majesty clothe You / Light and radiance cover You //
You stretch the curtain of the skies / You lay the beams of Your Chambers //
God makes the clouds His Chariot / He walks on the wings of the wind //
God made the mighty cherubim / He formed the fiery seraphim //
Laid the foundations of the Earth / That it should never be removed //
You blanketed Earth with oceans / Waters covered the highest peaks //
When You spoke, the floods retreated / At Your Thundering Voice they fled //
The rivers go up the mountains / The rivers go down the valleys //
The rivers go to hidden streams / Where You created the waters //
You set just how far they should go / No more shall the Earth overflow //
God sends the springs to the valleys / Sparkling springs which run through the hills //
They water the beasts of the field / Wild animals do drink their fill //
By the waters do the birds live / Singing among the river trees //
He sends the waters to the hills / Your fruitful work supplies their needs //
You make the grass grow for cattle / You make the herd grow for mankind //
That he might bring food from the Earth / And wine that cheers the heart with mirth //
And oil which makes the face to shine / And bread which brings strength to the heart //
The trees of the Lord give their sap / From the cedars of Lebanon //
The birds of the field build their nests / In the firs the stork builds her home //
Wild goats domicile in the hills / Feeble conies among the rocks //

The moon He gives for a night light / Sunrise and sunset, dawn to dusk //
Lord, You make the dark of the night / Forest beasts that roam in the night //
Young lions roar after their prey / God gives them their meat night by night //
At sunrise they gather themselves / And lay themselves down in their dens //
In the morning man goes to work / In the evening man returns home //
Lord, how manifold are Your Works! / You have made them all in Wisdom //
You have filled the Earth with riches / The Sea with creatures small and great //
The ships set out to ply their trade / And there Leviathan does play //
All of these do wait upon You / You give their meat when it is due //
What You give them, they gather in / Your Hand fills them without, within //
When You hide Your Face they tremble / When You take their breath they perish //
They all return unto the dust / Your Spirit of Creation sent //
Renews the face of the whole Earth / Your Glory that endures always //
Brings satisfaction to Your Work / And You rejoice in all Your Works //
God looks on Earth, and Earth trembles / God touches hills, and hills breathe smoke //
I will sing unto the Lord God / As long as I live I will sing //
I will sing praise unto my God / As long as I live I will sing //
I will meditate so sweetly / Be glad in the Lord completely //
Those who continue in their sins / Shall be consumed not to rise again //
And wicked souls who live therein / Shall be destroyed, no more to live //
I will bless the Lord, Oh my soul / Praise ye the Lord, Oh my soul

CHAPTER 105
"Give Thanks"

Give thanks unto the Lord / Call upon His Name / Make His Deeds to be known / Sing to Him with song //

Sing to Him with the psalms / Declare His Wonders / Glory unto His Name / Let the seekers come //

With joyful hearts of praise / Seekers seek the Lord / Seek the Lord and His Strength / Seek His Face always //

Remember His Marvels / Wonders and Judgments / Children of Abraham / Children of Jacob //

He is the Lord our God / His Judgments rule Earth / His Covenant Promise / Is not forgotten //

His oath to Abraham / Israel and Jacob / Confirmed unto Jacob / By way of a law //

And unto Israel / An eternal promise / I will give you Canaan / Your inheritance //

They were but a few men / Strangers were with them / Nation unto nation / People to people //

He let no man touch them / Reproved kings for them / Touch not mine anointed / Leave my prophets be //

He brought a great famine / Cut off bread supplies / Sent a man unto them / Joseph the slave man //

Shackles upon his feet / The Lord tested him / The king sent and loosed him / He let him go free //

Made him lord of his house / Lord of his substance / Lord of his senators / Lord of his princes //

Israel in Egypt / In the tents of Ham / Was increased by God much / Over all their foes //

God turned Egypt away / To hate His People / To deal deceitfully / Moses and Aaron //

Were chosen before them / Signs and wonders shown / He turned daylight to dark / They did not rebel //

He turned waters to blood / He sent a plague of frogs / Within and without / He sent a plague of flies //

They could not get out / He sent a plague of lice / They could not stop them / He sent a plague of hail //

Great stones mixed with fire / He killed their vines and figs / And their wasted trees / And then the locusts came //
Caterpillars, too / They could not count them all / They ate their herbs and fruit / The firstborn in the land //
Of man and beast / The chief of all their strength / They all were deceased / God brought His Children out //
With not one feeble soul / When He delivered / Egypt was glad they left / For the fear of them //
Pillar of cloud and fire / Gave cover and light / When they asked, He sent quail / Bread of Heaven, too //
Brought water from a rock / They drank, and they knew / Rushing, gushing water / Out in the desert //
God remembered His Word / His Holy Promise / He made to Abraham / And his descendants //
He brought them out with joy / His people were glad / He gave them heathen lands / Other men's labors //
That they might keep His Laws / Observe His Statutes / Praise be unto the Lord / Oh, praise ye the Lord

CHAPTER 106

"His Mercy is Forever"

Praise ye the Lord / Give thanks unto the Lord / For He is good / And His Mercy is forever //
Who can tell Him / Utter His Mighty Acts / Give praise to Him / There is more than can be given //
Keep sound judgment / Be righteous at all times / Remember me / Oh Lord, with favor and salvation //
Let me see good / That my soul may rejoice / For Your Nation / That I may with them rejoice //
We have all sinned / Our fathers before us sinned / Iniquity / We have done, and done wickedly //
They did not know / Your Egyptian Marvels / They did not see / The many times You showed Mercy //
They provoked God / At the sea, the Red Sea / But He saved them / From the hand of their enemies //

He redeemed them / From those who hated them / For His Name's Sake / He saved them to show His Power //

Rebuked the sea / The Red Sea turned dry land / He brought them out / Through the dry sea bed by His Hand //

As through desert / He saved them from evil / And redeemed them / From the hand of their enemies //

God drowned their foes / The waters covered them / Not one was left / Then did God's Children believe Him //

They sang praises / But forgot how He blessed / They listened not / But lusted in the wilderness //

They tempted God / He answered their request / Their soul suffered / They envied Aaron and Moses //

The earth opened / Swallowed Dathan alive / And Abiram / None of his family survived //

A fire started / The wicked were destroyed / The golden calf / They worshipped the golden image //

Their worship changed / From God to false idols / They forgot God / Who delivered them from Egypt //

Miracles there / Awesome through the Red Sea / God was angry / But Moses stood within the breech //

God's Anger gone / He did not destroy them / But they lacked faith / They murmured, complained against Him //

They listened not / To the Voice of the Lord / He turned from them / They wandered in the wilderness //

He scattered them / Among many nations / Overthrew them / In the midst of the wilderness //

They worshipped Baal / Sacrificed to the dead / They provoked Him / He sent the plague to humble them //

Phinehas stood / To fulfill God's Judgment / The plague was stopped / God blessed Phinehas forever //

They angered Him / At the waters of strife / At Meribah / Moses was provoked and angry //

His temper flared / He lost his composure / Spoke nasty words / Moses lost the right to cross over //

Their foes remained / Of whom God had spoken / Mingled with them / They learned the works of the heathen //

They served false gods / Which were a trap to them / They shed innocent blood / Their sons and daughters were given //
Were sacrificed / To Canaanite idols / The land unclean / Because of their idolatry //
They were defiled / They stirred up the Lord's Wrath / They were reviled / By the Lord who created them //
The heathen ruled / Nations that hated them / Did oppress them / And bring them under subjection //
God delivered / They provoked Him again / Evil counsel / Enslaved them in iniquity //
But He loved them / And heard them when they cried / He remembered / His Covenant, and changed His Mind //
He had pity / Caused them to be Pitied / He showed Mercy / Made their captors show them mercy //
Save us, Oh Lord / Save us and gather us / From all nations / And we will give thanks to You, Lord //
We will give thanks / Unto Your Holy Name / We will praise You / We will praise Your Name in triumph //
Blessed be the Lord / The God of Israel / From first to last / From forever to forever //
All the people / Let all the people say / Every one / Let all the people say Amen // Praise ye the Lord

CHAPTER 107

"Oh, That Men Would Praise the Lord"

Oh give thanks unto the Lord / God is a good God / His Mercy is forever / His redeemed souls speak //
Redeemed from the enemy / Gathered from all points / He has gathered from the east / Gathered from the west //
He has gathered from the north / Gathered from the south / The wilderness wanderers / Lonely and afraid //
Found no city to take them / Lacking food and drink / Their soul was ready to die / Then they cried to God //
He delivered from distress / Showed them the right path / Habitation and fortress / They crossed over there //

Oh, that men would praise the Lord / God is a good God / God is a merciful God / He fills longing souls //

Gives hungry souls His Goodness / In darkness and death / They are chained to affliction / Shackles chafe their skin //

They would not take God's counsel / His words they condemned / He broke their heart with labor / They fell down alone //

None was able to help them / Then they cried to God / He delivered from distress / From darkness to light //

From death's shadow to life's glow / He loosed their shackles / Oh, that men would praise the Lord / God is a good God //

God is a merciful God / Let them sacrifice / Offerings of thanksgiving / Praise and rejoicing //

Sailors and wayfaring men / See the works of God / And His wonders in the deep / He commands the wind //

The wind lifts a stormy gale / Rising to Heaven / Then down again unto Hell / They sway back and forth //

Staggering like a drunkard / Unable to tell / Completely at their wit's end / Then they cry to God //

He delivers from distress / He makes the storm cease / Calls the stormy waves to peace / They are now quiet //

They make landfall in safe haven / Their destination / Oh that men would praise the Lord / God is a good God //

God is a merciful God / Let them exalt Him / In the great congregation / And give praise to Him //

Where the elders congregate / Rivers to deserts / He turns springs to dry ground / Fruitful to barren //

When evil men are around / Wilderness to wells / Dry ground turned to water springs / The hungry dwell there //

They prepare cities to live / They sow the fields there / And prepare vineyards all around / Which yield their fruits there //

He gives them blessing also / They are multiplied / Their cattle are protected / He brings the proud low //

Through affliction and sorrow / Oppresses princes / With wilderness wanderings / Where there is no way //

But He sets the poor on high / From all affliction / Prepares for their families / Like a flock of sheep //

The righteous shall see this, and / Rejoice in God's Grace / Evil men shall be silent / With nothing to say //

Whoever is wise will see / Observing these things / The Loving Kindness of God / To humanity

CHAPTER 108
"Be Exalted, Oh, Lord"

My heart is fixed on You / I will sing Your Praise, Lord / With all of my heart / Psaltery and harp //

I will awake early / Oh Lord, I will praise Thee / Among the nations / Your Mercy is great //

Above the heavenlies / Your Truth reaches the skies / Better Heaven and Earth / Better Mercy and Truth //

Be exalted Oh Lord / Far above the heavens / Let Your Glory shine / Far above the earth //

Bring out Your Beloved / With Your Hand of Power / Hear me when I call / Hear me and answer //

God speaks in Holiness / With Joy is Righteousness / I will split Shechem / And Succoth valley //

Gilead's My Land / Manasseh is My Land / Strength of Ephraim / Lawgiver, Judah //

Moab is My Washpot / Edom is My Carpet / Philistia is / My Place of Triumph //

How can I reach Edom / Who will lead me inside / The city of strength / Lord God of all Strength //

Will You not lead me there / Into the battle / Give us help from trouble / For man cannot help us //

Through God we shall fight / Victoriously / He is the One who / Treads down our enemies

CHAPTER 109
"The Strength of the Poor"

Do not be quiet, praiseworthy God / Wicked deceitful men rail on me / Their lying tongues conspire against me / With fateful words they surrounded me //

Without a reason they battled me / They are adversaries against love / Yet I continue to pray for them / They gave evil for good, hate for love //

Appoint a wicked ruler for them / With Satan the strength behind His Throne / When judgment comes, let him be condemned / And turn his every prayer to sin //

Do not extend his days of power / Let a stranger occupy his place / Let his children be without a father / And let his wife be without husband //

Let his children always be begging / In loneliness let them be begging / Let the extortioner catch his pay / Let strangers take his labor away //

Let usual mercies be denied / Let his orphans lose favor and pride / Let his heirs be cut off from all grace / Let his family name be erased //

Let the sins of his fathers be judged / Let the sins of his mother be judged / Let their sin remain before the Lord / That He may cut off their heritage //

Because he refused to show mercy / But came against the poor and needy / He sought to slay the heartbroken souls / As he cursed, let cursing come to him //

As he blessed not, let him not be blessed / As cursing covered him like a robe / Let cursing enter him like water / Let it enter in his bones like oil //

Let cursing be for his covering / For his girdle continually / Let God thus reward my enemies / And those who plot evil against me //

But have Mercy on me, Oh Lord God / Deliver me because of Your Name / I am poor and in need of Your Help / My broken heart in need of Your Help //

I have fasted and weakened my knees / My health is broken through much fasting / I am reproached by my enemies / They shook their heads when they looked at me //

Oh Lord my God, please save and help me / According to Your Tender Mercy / That they may know this is Your Hand, Lord / That they may know that You did this, Lord //

Let them curse, but bless me for Your Name / When they arise, let them be ashamed / But let Your Servant rejoice with joy / Let my foes be clothed with their own shame //
Let their mantle be a confused face / With my mouth I will greatly praise God / Among all people I will praise God / He shall be the Strength of the poor // To save him to be condemned no more

CHAPTER 110
"The Rod of Your Strength"

The Spirit spoke to my Lord / Sit at the Right Hand of Power / Your foes shall be Your Footstool / You shall send the Rod of Your Strength //
Out of Zion You shall rule / Your people shall rejoice in You / In the day of Your Power / More than the early morning glow //
Holy Beauties of God show / With youthful radiance You Shine / The Lord has made this promise / You are a priest forever //
As was Melchizedek / God in the Power of His Might / Shall slay great kings in anger / He shall judge among all nations //
Dead bodies fill the spaces / He shall wound many heads of state / Drink of the brook by the way / He shall lift His Head in Power

CHAPTER 111
"I Am in Praise Wholehearted"

Praise ye the Lord God of Hosts / I am in praise wholehearted / In the righteous assembly / In the great congregation //
The Lord works many great works / Sought by all who love His Works / His work is full of honor / His Work is full of Glory //
The Lord my God is Righteous / The Lord my God is Holy / Forever His Works shall stand / The Lord gives Grace by His Hand //
A compassionate Friend, He / Has fed all those who fear Him / He will keep His Covenant / He showed His People His Might //
Giving them their heritage / Among all Nations His Works / Are true, His Commandments right / Righteous Truth from God shall be //

Standing for eternity / He sent His Redemption Plan / His Covenant always stands / He is Holy and Revered //

All who lack wisdom should fear / God the Author of Wisdom / Understanding follows all / Who obey His Commandments //

His Praise endures forever

CHAPTER 112
"The Generation of the Righteous"

Praise be to the Lord God / Blessed is the man who fears Him / Who rejoices in His Commands / His descendants shall have much power //

The generation of the righteous / Shall be blessed with wealth and richness / His righteousness shall remain / His light shines in the dark //

He is full of grace, and / He is full of compassion / He is righteous, shows good favor / He lends to others with discretion //

He shall be remembered forever / His righteousness shall not be moved / He shall not fear evil news / His heart trusts in the Lord //

His heart is established / He shall never be afraid / Until his enemies perish / He has helped the poor needy people //

His righteousness is known forever / His strength shall grow with great honor / Evil men grieve, gnash their teeth / Their desire shall perish

CHAPTER 113
"His Glory is Above All"

All ye people, praise the Lord / Praise Him, Servants of the Lord / Praise the great Name of the Lord / Sunrise sunset praise the Lord //

The Lord is High above all / His Glory is above all / Above all Heaven and Earth / The Lord God has matchless Worth //

Who looks down to see Heaven / Humbles himself to see Earth / He lifts poor and needy souls / Out of the dunghill and dirt //

He sets him with the princes / The princes of His People / Barrenness to mother's joy / He makes the barren keep house //

Even though she wastes in grief / He gives children and relief / All ye people, praise the Lord

CHAPTER 114
"Trembling at the Presence of the Lord"

When Israel departed Egypt / The house of Jacob from slavery / From a people of another tongue / Judah was the Lord's Sanctuary //

Israel was the Lord's Dominion / The sea saw the Presence of the Lord / Red Sea fled the Presence of the Lord / The Jordan River saw His Presence //

The Jordan stood at the Lord's Presence / Mountains skipped like rams at His Presence / Little hills like lambs at His Presence / Red Sea, Red Sea, what made you flee? //

Jordan River, what made you stand? / Mountains what made you skip like the rams? / Little hills, what made you skip like lambs? / Trembling at the Presence of the Lord //

The Presence of the God of Jacob / Who turned the rock to standing water / The flint to a fountain of waters

CHAPTER 115
"Trust in The Lord"

Not because of us, Oh Lord God / It is not because of us / Because of Your Name give glory / For Your Great Mercy and Truth //

Why should the heathen nations say / Wherefore did their God leave them? / But our God is in the heavens / He has done as it pleased Him //

The idols of the nations are / Silver and gold made by man / They have eyes unable to see / They have ears unable to hear //

They have noses that cannot smell / They have hands that do not feel / They have feet unable to walk / They have mouths that do not talk //

They that make them are just like them / So are all who trust in them / Oh Israel, trust in the Lord / He is their Help, and their Shield //

House of Aaron, trust in the Lord / He is their Help, and their Shield / You who fear the Lord, trust in Him / He is their Help, and their Shield //

The Lord has been mindful of us / God Almighty will bless us / Blessing the house of Israel / Blessing the house of Aaron //

He will bless those who fear the Lord / He will bless both great and small / He will bless you and your children / Give increase unto you all //

The Lord who made Heaven and Earth / You are blessed of that same Lord / Heaven belongs to the Lord God / Earth to the children of men //

The dead cannot praise the Lord God / Those in the grave speak no more / But we will raise a praise to Him / Both now, and forevermore //

All who trust in Him, praise the Lord / All His Children praise the Lord

CHAPTER 116
"What Can I Give Back to The Lord?"

I sought the Lord, He heard my cry / Answered my supplications / I will call upon the Lord in / Every situation //

For as long as I live, I know / The pains of death and sorrow / Had almost taken me under / Hell brought trouble and sorrow //

Then I called the Name of the Lord / Lord, please deliver my soul / The Lord is Righteous at all times / He is Gracious, Merciful //

The simple soul is saved by Him / I was low in station, poor / In my low estate I called Him / He sent my help and comfort //

Rest in the Lord God, Oh my soul / He has given you bounty / My soul from death, my eyes from tears / My feet from falling, all these //

I will walk in His Sweet Presence / For as long as I shall live / In my faith my mouth has spoken / Once afflicted, yet I live //

In my haste, false words were spoken / None would be true, none would give / What can I give back to the Lord? / For all He has done for me //

I will enjoy His Salvation / And call on His Name daily / I will fulfill my promises / That I have made to the Lord //

In the presence of the people / Shall I bring my offerings / Precious in the sight of the Lord / Priceless worth beyond measure //

Is the death of each of His Saints / More than all hidden treasure / Lord, I am Your Servant in truth / My mother was Your Handmaid //

You have loosed my soul from bondage / Your thanksgiving I will raise / With much thanksgiving will I call / Upon Your Great and Holy Name //

I will fulfill my promises / That I have made to the Lord / In the presence of His People / Shall I bring my offerings //

In the courts of Your House, Oh Lord / City of Jerusalem / I will give praise unto the Lord / All praise be unto the Lord

CHAPTER 117
"God's Eternal Love and Truth"

Oh, give praise unto the Lord / All Nations of the world / Praise the Lord, all ye people / Let His Banner be unfurled //

God's eternal Love and Truth / Overtake us from the womb / Childhood, youth, up through old age / Merciful Kindness is great //

For as long as we shall live / Praises unto Him we give / Praise the Lord, all ye people / Let all people praise ye the Lord

CHAPTER 118
"His Mercy Endures Forever"

Oh, give thanks unto the good Lord, for / His mercy endures forever / Let the nation of Israel say / His mercy endures forever //

Let all of the House of Aaron say / His mercy endures forever / Let all them that fear the Lord now say / His mercy endures forever //

I called upon the Lord in trouble / He answered me on the double / He set me in a place with much room / I will not fear what man can do //

The Lord Almighty is on my side / What is it man can do to me? / The Lord gives help to them who help me / The Lord shall hate them who hate me //

It is better to trust in the Lord / Than to put your trust in princes / Every nation surrounded me / In His Name I will destroy them //

Together they all surrounded me / They came together against me / But in His Name I will destroy them / They compassed me like a swarm of bees //

They are put out like fire among thorns / For in God's name I will quench them / The enemy has thrust against me / Attempting to cause me to fall //

The Lord is my Strength, the Song I sing, / And my Salvation on the wing / Voices of joy, songs of salvation / Sound in the tents of the righteous //

The Strong Hand of the Lord Almighty / Works with strength most valiantly / The Strength of the Lord is exalted / The Strength of the Lord is valiant //

I shall not die, but I shall live to / Declare the mighty Works of the Lord / The Lord has disciplined me sorely / But the enemy cannot kill me //

When the gates of righteousness open / I will praise the Lord in the gates / In the gate where the righteous enter / I will praise You within that place //

For You have answered my earnest prayer / And become my Salvation there / The Stone which the builders rejected / Has become the Chief Cornerstone //

This is the Work of the Lord of Hosts / It is miraculous to us / This is the Day that the Lord has made / With joy we will be glad in it //

Save us and send us prosperity / Oh Lord, our Lord God Almighty / Blessed is he that cometh in Your Name / Out of the house of God we bless //

God is the Lord who gave us the light / With cords, the sacrifice we bind / You are my God, and I will praise You / You are my God, I will exalt //

Oh, give thanks unto the good Lord, for / His Mercy endures forever

CHAPTER 119
"Overview"

Chapter 119: "Psalms 119, Overview"
Chapter 119: "A Heart Not Divided" (Alef)
Chapter 119: "A Word Not Forgotten" (Bet)
Chapter 119: "A Law Not Forsaken" (Gimel)
Chapter 119: "A Soul Not Embittered" (Dalet)
Chapter 119: "A Mind Not Corrupted" (Heh)
Chapter 119: "A Trust Not Unfounded" (Vav)
Chapter 119: "A Hope Not Divided" (Zayin)
Chapter 119: "A Way Not Abandoned" (Het)
Chapter 119: "A Life Not Unchanging" (Tet)
Chapter 119: "A Hand Not Unfaithful" (Yud)
Chapter 119: "A Love Not Uncaring" (Kaf)
Chapter 119: "A Faith Not Retiring" (Lamed)
Chapter 119: "A Taste Not Overlooked" (Mem)
Chapter 119: "A Path Not Unlighted" (Nun)
Chapter 119: "A Shield Not Unpolished" (Samekh)
Chapter 119: "A Rule Not Devalued" (Ayin)
Chapter 119: "A Step Not Unordered" (Peh)
Chapter 119: "A Zeal Not Abated" (Tzadeh)
Chapter 119: "A Voice Not Wavering" (Kuf)
Chapter 119: "A Truth Not Stoppable" (Resh)
Chapter 119: "A Stand Not Changeable" (Shin)
Chapter 119: "A Soul Not Separate" (Tav)

CHAPTER 119 (ALEF)
"A Heart Not Divided"

Blessed are they who walk in the Law / Of the Lord with sincerity / Blessed are the wholehearted seekers / Who keep the Lord's Testimonies // Blessed are they who walk in His Ways / Keeping far from iniquity / You have given a clear command to / Keep Your Precepts diligently //

Lord, I pray You to direct my ways / To Keep Your Statutes for always / I shall never have to be ashamed / When I respect Your Commandments //

I will praise You with an upright heart / When I learn Your Righteous Rule of Law / Your Statutes I will daily obey / Lord, forsake me not out of the way

CHAPTER 119 (BET)
"A Word Not Forgotten"

Where is the power / For a young man / To live a clean life? / By taking Your Word first //

With all of my heart / I have sought You / Let me not stray from, / The Commands that You gave / I have hid Your Word / In a safe place / Deep within my heart / Where sin may be erased //

Blessed are You Lord / Teach Your Statutes / I willingly learn / I have declared Your Truth //

Your Righteous Judgments / Have I declared / I have rejoiced in / Your Testimonies, Lord //

More than wealth to me / In Your Precepts / I will meditate / And I will give honor //

To all of Your Ways / Your Statutes are / My sincere delight / And Your Word day and night

CHAPTER 119 (GIMEL)
"A Law Not Forsaken"

Deal bountifully with me / That I may live Your Word to keep / Give me eyes that I may see / The wonders Your Law shows me / I am a wanderer here / Show me Your Commandments so clear / My soul breaks the while it waits / For your Judgments You will relate //

You rebuked the proud, cursed souls / Who left Your Commands and were bold / Take reproach, contempt from me / I obeyed Your Testimonies //

Princes spoke ill against me / But I did meditate on Thee / Your Statutes, perfect and right / Your Testimonies, my delight //

They counsel me day and night / That my steps are true and upright

CHAPTER 119 (DALET)
"A Soul Not Embittered"

My soul is cleaving unto the dust / Enliven me, Your Word I trust / I have spoken my ways before You / You have heard, so teach me Your Statutes //

Your Precepts I need understanding / I shall speak of Your Works outstanding / My soul drops with a heavy burden / When Your Word comes, my soul is strengthened //

Keep me from the path of all lying / Graciously Your Law supplying / Your Truth is the path that I shall seek / Your Judgments have I set before me //

Unto Your Testimonies I cling / Oh Lord, let not shame be put to me / Enlarge my heart so that I might stand / And I will run after Your Commands

CHAPTER 119 (HEH)
"A Mind Not Corrupted"

Teach me, Oh Lord / How Your Statutes work / Keep them in my mind / And I will not shirk //

Help me understand / I shall keep Your Law / I shall observe it / Heart, soul, mind, strength-all / Take me to the path / Of Your Commandments / I delight in them / I shall observe them //

Align my heart with / Your Testimonies / Covetousness I / Shall keep far from me //

Keep vain thoughts from me / Keep me in Your Way / Show Your Word to me / Godly fear each day //

Keep me from reproach / Your Justice is good / Your Precepts I need / Righteousness Godspeed

CHAPTER 119 (VAV)
"A Trust Not Unfounded"

Let Your Mercies come to me, Oh Lord / Even Your Salvation, from Your Word / Give me answers to them that reproach / A trust not unfounded, Your Word holds //

Do not take Your Word of truth from me / I hope in Your Justice, this I plea / I shall keep Your Law continually / And forever walk in liberty / Your Precepts I seek in everything / Your Testimonies sure I will speak / Before kings, and will not be ashamed / Of Your Commands spoken in Your Name //

Your Commands my hands also lift up / I think on Your Laws, which I have loved

CHAPTER 119 (ZAYIN)
"A Hope Not Divided"

Remember the Word You promised me / Which gives me a hope not divided / This my comfort in my affliction / Is Your Word which makes me enlivened //

The proud have heaped derision on me / Yet I remain faithful to Your Law / I remember Judgments of old / I am comforted by them in all //

Many furies take hold of my mind / For the wicked that forsake Your Law / Your Statutes are songs of hope to me / Wherever I live, Your Ways bring peace //

I have called Your Name in darkest night / Your Law is a comfort and delight / I have kept Your Precepts in my soul / For this my hope keeps me free and whole

CHAPTER 119 (HET)
"A Way Not Abandoned"

You are my portion, Oh Lord my God / I have promised I would keep Your Words / I have sought Your Face with my whole heart / Have Mercy according to Your Word //

I thought, I turned, then I testified / Made no delay to keep Your Commands / Companies of wicked thieves robbed me / But I kept in mind Your Righteous Law //
At midnight I thank You for justice / I befriend those who keep Your Precepts / And all who revere the Almighty / You fill the Earth with Mercy and Grace //
Teach me Your Laws in Your Secret Place

CHAPTER 119 (TET)
"A Life Not Unchanging"

You have treated me well, Oh Lord / According to Your Promise / Teach me good wisdom and knowledge / I have trusted in Your Commands //
Before I was humbled I sinned / But now I keep Your Word once more / Lord, You are good and do good things / Teach me Your Laws, just as before //
Proud lies have risen against me / Your Precepts my whole heart will keep / Their heart is fat with their own grease / But in Your Law my heart delights //
Lord, You have humbled me for good / That I might learn Your Statutes well / Lord, the Law that comes from Your Mouth / Is better than all worldly wealth

CHAPTER 119 (YUD)
"A Hand Not Unfaithful"

Your Hands have formed and fashioned me / Help me understand Your Commands / Those who fear Thee joy to see me / Because my hope is in Your Plan / Your Judgments are true and faithful / A hand not unfaithful touched me / You were right when You afflicted / In faithfulness You humbled me //
I pray You let Your Kind Mercy / Come to comfort me by Your Word / Let Your Tender Mercies find me / That I may live to love Your Law //

Let all the proud ones be ashamed / Who reviled me without a cause / But I will observe Your Precepts / Let those who revere Thee join me //
Rejoice in Your Testimonies / As all those who have known them do / Purify me in Your Statutes / And I will not be shamed by You

CHAPTER 119 (KAF)
"A Love Not Uncaring"

My soul faints for Your Salvation / My hope is in Your Word of Truth / My eyes search until they are dim / A love not uncaring come in //
As a wineskin trapped in the smoke / I shrink, and yet do not forget / Your Statutes for how many days / I wait for justice to be set / The wicked persecute me now / Proud men have dug pits for my soul / They do not follow after Law / Although Your Commands are faithful //
They persecute me with no cause / Help me, Lord, that I may yet live / I was almost removed from Earth / But Your Precepts I would not leave //
Oh Lord God Almighty keep me / Alive in Your Lovingkindness / I will keep Your Testimony / The Testimony of Your Mouth

CHAPTER 119 (LAMED)
"A Faith Not Retiring"

Your Word, Oh Lord is forever / Your Word is settled in Heaven / Your Faithfulness to the whole Earth //
Is unto all generations / You have established the whole Earth / The whole Earth abides forever //
The inhabitants thereof live / By Your Ordinances they live / You give all living things their life //
Unless Your Law had been my love / My humbling should have been my death / I shall not forget Your Precepts / You used Your Precepts to save me / With Your Precepts You quickened me / Lord, I am Your Servant: save me! //

I have sought Your Precepts, Oh God / The wicked laid wait for my soul / But Your Testimonies I know //
I see an end to perfection / But Your Commandment has no end / A faith not retiring at all

CHAPTER 119 (MEM)
"A Taste Not Overlooked"

Oh how much I love Your Law / I meditate therein all day / Your Commandments have made me wise / Wiser than all my enemies //
Your Commands are always with me / My understanding is greater / Than my teachers could have shown me / I think on Your Testimonies //
I know more than the ancients knew / Because I keep Your Precepts too / I have kept myself from evil / That I might keep Your Holy Word //
I have stayed true to Your Judgments / Lord, You have taught me their value / Your Words a taste not overlooked / More sweet than honey in my mouth //
Your Precepts help me understand / Until every false way is banned

CHAPTER 119 (NUN)
"A Path Not Unlighted"

Your Word is a Lamp to my feet / Your Word is a Light to my path / A path not unlighted is mine / I made a promise I will keep //
I will keep Your Judgments of Truth / I am humbled by affliction / Lord, enliven me by Your Word / Accept my freewill offerings //
And to my path Your Judgments bring / Lord, my soul is Yours to command / And I keep Your Law close at hand / The wicked set a trap for me //
Yet in Your Precepts I will be / Your Testimonies do I take / A heritage for me they make / They make my heart happy and glad //
To Your Laws I incline my heart / Even to the end impart

CHAPTER 119 (SAMEKH)
"A Shield Not Unpolished"

I hate all vanity / But Your Law do I love / You are my Hiding Place / A Shield not unpolished //
Lord, Your Word is my hope / Leave me, evil doers / I will keep God's commands / Hold me up in Your Word //
And I shall live, not die / Let me not be ashamed / My hope is not in vain / Hold me up, make me safe //
I respect Your Laws always / You trod down those who leave / Your Law, that Your soul grieves / Their lies are grief to You //
You cease the things they do / As silver dross removed / I love to testify / Of Your Testimonies //
I stand in awe of You / I fear Your Judgments, too

CHAPTER 119 (AYIN)
"A Rule Not Devalued"

I have ruled in truth and justice / Leave me not to my oppressors / Stand up for me, for my soul's good / Let not oppression take the good //
My eyes fail for Your Salvation / Your Right Words to all the nations / Please treat with me in Your Mercy / Your Statutes I need You to teach //
I am Yours, help me understand / Your Testimonies by Your Hands / Lord, it is time for You to work / Evil men have voided Your Work //
Your Commandments are more than gold / They mean more to me than fine gold / Your Precepts in all things are right / I hate all false ways day and night

CHAPTER 119 (PEH)
"A Step Not Unordered"

Your Covenants are filled with wonder / My soul keeps them over and under / The entrance of Your Words lights the soul / Understanding simply takes control //

I panted like a deer for Your Word / Longing for Your Commands to be heard / Look upon me in Mercy, dear Lord / As You did for those who love Your Name / A step not unordered will You give / Break iniquity with its dark chains / Deliver me from man's oppression / And so I will keep all Your Precepts //

Cause Your Face to radiate on me / Teach me Your Statutes that will keep me / I cry rivers of tears from my eyes / When I find Your Laws they do not keep

CHAPTER 119 (TZADEH)
"A Zeal Not Abated"

You are righteous, Oh Lord / And Your Justice is right / Your Testimonies right / Your Commandments are right / All of these are righteous / All of these are faithful / A zeal not abated / Has taken hold of me //

Because my enemies / Have ignored Your Words, Lord / Your Word is very pure / I love Your Word of truth //

Insignificant, I / Yet Your Precepts are mine / Righteousness forever / Clings to Your Law of truth //

Trouble has taken me / Anguish has taken me / Yet Your Commands I love / Lord, Your Testimonies //

Are righteous forever / Help me understand them / And I shall live by them

CHAPTER 119 (KUF)
"A Voice Not Wavering"

Wholeheartedly I cried / A voice not wavering / Lord hear me when I cry / Your Laws I will obey //

I cried Lord please save me / I shall obey Your Word / Your Covenants to keep / Your Testimonies heard //
I came before the dawn / In hope I sought Your Word / I come before the night / Meditate on Your Word //
Lord hear me when I pray / In lovingkindness speak / That I may quickly know / Your Justice that I seek //
My enemies draw near / Yet they are far from You / Your Law they will not hear / Even though You are near //
And Your Commands are true / About Your Covenants / All Your Testimonies / And Your Salvation Plan //
You taught me long ago / From beginning to end / Established forever / You gave these unto man

CHAPTER 119 (RESH)
"A Truth Not Stoppable"

I am afflicted, Lord / Consider, Deliver / I keep in mind Your Law / Plead my case, Deliver //
Make me quick in Your Word / Evil men are not saved / For they seek not Your Ways / Your Law is far from them //
They will not seek Your Face / Your Tender Mercies, Lord / Are many and wondrous / Make me quick in Your Law //
To learn of Your Justice / My persecutors come / My enemies are near / Your Testimonies are //
To me yet very dear / The transgressors grieved me / I saw that they were weak / They would not keep Your Word //
Your Truth they did not seek / Consider my love, Lord / Your Precepts bring me life / Enliven me, Oh Lord //
Be loving and be kind / In the beginning, God / Your Word is true and right / Your Righteous Justice reigns //
Forevermore in sight

CHAPTER 119 (SHIN)
"A Stand Not Changeable"

Princes persecute me / They have not a reason / A stand not changeable / Have I in Thy Word //
I stand in awe of it / I rejoice at Thy Word / Treasures great are in it / I abhor all lying //
But Thy Law do I love / I praise Thee seven times / Within each passing day / Because of Righteousness //
Your Justice leads the way / Great peace has every one / Who loves Your Law above / Nothing shall offend them //
They are kept in Your Love / Lord, I have hoped in You / For Your Great Salvation / And followed Your Commands //
Your Testimonies kept / I love them very much / Your Precepts I have kept / Your Testimonies loved //
All my ways before You / Are known from up above

CHAPTER 119 (TAV)
"A Soul Not Separate"

Let my cry come to You / Lord, help me know Your Word / My supplication near / Deliverance so dear //
My lips shall utter praise / Your Statutes I will raise / My tongue shall tell Your Word / All Your Commands are right //
Let Your Hand help me win / Your Precepts I did choose / I need Your Salvation / Your Law is my delight //
My soul Your Name shall praise / Your Justice gives me help / Like a lost sheep I strayed / I could not help myself //
Seek and save Your Servant / I think on Your Commands / A soul not separate / From Your Commands I am

CHAPTER 120
"Deliverance from Deceit"

In my distress I cried out / To God, and He heard my cry / Deliverance from deceit / And from evil lips that lie //

What possible remedy / What shall be done unto thee / Who speakest with a false tongue / A mighty man with arrows //

And red hot juniper coals / Woe is me if I sojourn / In Mesech or in Kedar / My neighbors are not for peace //

When I speak, they are for war

CHAPTER 121
"Soul Preserver"

I will look toward the hills / This is the place of my help / God is the source of my help / Maker of Heaven and Earth //

He will not let your foot slip / He who keeps you will not slip / Israel's keeper will not / Slumber or sleep, and He keeps //

Your soul, and shades your right hand / The daytime sun will not strike / Neither the moon strike at night / He will keep you from evil //

He is your Soul Preserver / The Lord shall preserve your soul / In and out, and up and down / The Lord is your Strength always

CHAPTER 122
"I Was Glad"

I was glad when they said unto me / Let us go to the House of the Lord / And our feet shall be standing in Thee / In Your Gates, Oh Great Jerusalem //

Where the Tribes of the Lord enter in / The testimony of Israel / To give thanks to the Name of the Lord / Thrones of judgment are set in the house / Thrones are set in the house of David / For the peace of Jerusalem pray / Those who love her shall prosper always / Peace be within Jerusalem's walls //

In her palaces, prosperity / For your kinsman and your close friends' sakes / I will say peace be within her gates / Because the House of the Lord is there //
I will seek her good from everywhere

CHAPTER 123
"Our Eyes Wait on The Lord Our God"

Unto You lift my eyes, Oh Lord / You who dwell in the skies above / Eyes of servants look to their masters / Eyes of maiden unto her mistress //
Our eyes wait on the Lord our God / Until He has Mercy on us / Have Mercy upon us evermore / For we are reproached with contempt / The proud souls are filled with contempt //
Our soul is filled to overflowing / With scorn from proud souls who live at ease

CHAPTER 124
"If God Had Not Been on Our Side"

If God had not been on our side / So may Israel say today / If God had not been on our side / When rose up all our enemies //
Then they had swallowed us alive / When they decided to attack / The waters overwhelming us / Were an impossibility //
Streams of damnation over us / Proud waters washed over our soul / All blessing be unto the Lord / Who keeps us from being their prey //
As a bird in a fowler's snare / Snare is broken, and we escaped / The Name of the Lord is our help / The Lord who made Heaven and Earth

CHAPTER 125
"The Lord Surrounds His People"

They that trust in the Lord / Shall be as Mount Zion / Which abides forevermore / Which cannot be removed //

As the mountains stand tall / About Jerusalem / The Lord surrounds His People / Forever they shall stand //
Wickedness shall not rest / On souls of the righteous / To teach them iniquity / The righteous follow Thee //

Lord help those who do good / And do good unto them / Do good to the upright souls / To those with upright hearts //
For those who turn aside / To take the crooked path / They shall be judged with sinners / Peace be to Israel

CHAPTER 126
"They That Sow in Tears"

When the Lord returned Zion / Returning from captivity / It was like a blissful dream / Laughter rang throughout the nation //
We were singing praise to Him / Then they said among the heathen / He has done great things for them / The Lord had done great things for us //
We rejoice in all He does / Turn us around again, Oh Lord / As the streams to the south turn / They that sow in tears shall reap a //
Harvest of joy forever / He that goes and sows with weeping / Precious seed bearers shall come / With joy be shall bring in his sheaves

CHAPTER 127
"Unless the Lord Builds the House"

Unless the Lord builds the house / They labor in vain who build it / Unless the Lord keeps the city / The watchman watches in vain //
It is vain to rise early / To sit up late just to worry / For so He gives His Children sleep / Children are His Heritage //
Children are the Lord's Reward / As arrows in a warrior's hand / So are the children of the youth / Happy is he with many //
And they shall not be ashamed / They shall speak with their enemies / With their enemies in the gate / They shall speak there with no fear

CHAPTER 128
"He That Fears the Lord"

Blessed are all who fear the Lord / Blessed are those who walk in His Ways / You shall receive of your work / You will be happy, treated well //

Your wife shall be most fruitful / As a vine on the trellis / Your children like olive plants / When they sit around the table //

Blessed is he that fears the Lord / Out of Zion He gives blessings / Good things from Jerusalem / For all of your days you shall see //

You shall see your grandchildren / The peace of Israel you seek

CHAPTER 129
"They Who Fought Me Did Not Win"

Many times have I been afflicted / From my youth, Israel may now say / Many times have they afflicted me / They who fought me did not win //

The plowers plowed stripes upon my back / They plowed their furrows with long, deep strokes / The Righteous Lord cut the wicked cords / Let them all be much reproached //

Those that hate Zion as housetop grass / The grass that withers before it grows / The mower has nothing left to mow / He who binds sheaves finds no grain //

Those who pass by the way cannot say / The blessing of the Lord be on you / We bless You in the name of the Lord / Man cannot bless what God cursed

CHAPTER 130
"Out of the Depths"

I have cried to You, Oh Lord / Out of the depths / Hear my supplications, Lord / Lord, hear my voice //

If you mark iniquities / Who should then stand? / But forgiveness is with Thee / Throughout the land //

My soul does wait for the Lord / I wait for Him / My soul does wait for the Lord / More than watchmen //

Who guard the city all night / Until morning / Let Israel hope in God / Who shows Mercy //

He has Redemption for all / Plenteously / He shall redeem Israel / From all his sins

CHAPTER 131
"Let Israel Hope in The Lord"

Lord, I do not have a haughty heart / Nor do I possess lofty eyes / Neither walk in mysteries / Wonderful things too high for me //

Surely I have quieted my soul / As a child weaned of his mother / My soul is as a weaned child / Let Israel hope in the Lord //

From this time forward forevermore

CHAPTER 132
"Lord, Remember David"

Lord, remember David / And all his afflictions / He swore unto the Lord / To the God of Jacob //

I will not enter in / My house, my home, my bed / Nor give sleep to my eyes / Slumber to my eyelids //

Until I find a place / Place of habitation / For the God of Jacob / Ephratah heard the Word //

It is in the Forest / In His Tabernacles / Worship at His Footstool / For Earth is His Footstool //

Arise to Your Rest, Lord / With the Ark of Your Strength / Let Your Priests be righteous / Let Your Saints be joyful //

For Your Servant David / Turn not away my face / The Lord promised David / He will not turn away //

Among his descendants / Would God set up His Throne / The Lord did choose Zion / For an habitation //

This is My Resting Place / This is where I will dwell / This is the Lord's Desire / Abundantly do dwell //

All of her provision / Bread to all the nations / I will bless her priesthood / Clothed in My Salvation //

Her saints shall shout for joy / The horn of David raised / A lamp for My Servant / His foes shall be ashamed / But His Crown shall be praised

CHAPTER 133
"The Ointment of Unity"

How good and pleasant it is / When brethren are together / The ointment of unity //

That is precious and costly / It is like that of Aaron / The ointment ran down his beard //

To the end of his priestly robe / As the dew of Mount Hermon / That fell upon Mount Zion //

The Lord commanded blessing / Even life forevermore / The ointment of unity

CHAPTER 134
"Bless Ye The Lord"

Behold, bless ye the Lord / All ye Servants of the Lord / Which by night stand in the Lord's House //

Raise your hands in the Sanctuary / Bless the Lord of Heaven and Earth / God who made all Heaven and Earth //

Bless thee out of Zion / All ye Servants of the Lord / Behold, bless ye the Lord

CHAPTER 135
"Praise Ye The Lord"

Praise ye the Lord, praise His Name, / Let the Servants of the Lord praise Him / Ye that stand in the House of the Lord / Ye that stand in the Courts of the Lord //

Praise ye the Lord, praise His Name / He is good, and it is pleasing / For the Lord chose Jacob for Himself / For the Lord chose Israel His Prize //

His peculiar treasure / For the Lord is great above all / Whatsoever the Lord pleased, He did / Heaven, Earth, the seas, the deep oceans //

The Lord sends the morning dew / The Lord makes the lightnings and rain / The Lord brings the wind out of hiding / The Lord smote the firstborn of Egypt //

The Lord smote both the man and beast / The Lord sent Egyptian wonders / Upon Pharaoh and all his servants / The Lord smote nations and kings alike //

Sihon, king of Amorites / And Og, the king of Bashan / He smote all the kingdoms of Canaan / And gave their land for a heritage //

To His People Israel / Your Name, Lord, endures forever / Your Memorial throughout all time / The Lord will come to judge His People //

The Lord will bless His Servants / Idols made of silver and gold / The idols of the heathen nations / They are all the work of some man's hands //

They have mouths yet cannot speak / They have ears but they cannot hear / They have noses but they cannot breathe / They that make them are like unto them //

So are all who trust in them / Bless the Lord, House of Israel / Bless the Lord, Oh ye House of Aaron / Bless the Lord, Oh ye House of Levi //

Bless the Lord, all ye that fear Him / Blessed be the Lord out of Zion / Bless the Lord, all at Jerusalem / Praise ye the Lord, children of the Lord

CHAPTER 136
"His Mercy Lasts Forever"

Oh give thanks unto the Lord / He is Good and Merciful / His Mercy lasts forever / Oh give thanks to the Lord God //

His Mercy lasts forever / By Wisdom He made the skies / His Mercy lasts forever / The Earth above the waters //

His Mercy lasts forever / To Him who made the great lights / His Mercy lasts forever / He made the sun for the day //

His Mercy lasts forever / The moon and stars for the night / His Mercy lasts forever / He smote all Egypt's firstborn //

His Mercy lasts forever / Took Israel from Egypt / His Mercy lasts forever / With strong hand and stretched out arm //

His Mercy lasts forever / He divided the Red Sea / His Mercy lasts forever / Made Israel cross over //

His Mercy lasts forever / Drowned Pharaoh and his army / His Mercy lasts forever / Led His People through desert //

His Mercy lasts forever / To Him who destroyed great kings / His Mercy lasts forever / Sihon of the Amorites //

His Mercy lasts forever / And Og the king of Bashan / His Mercy lasts forever / Gave their land to His People //

His Mercy lasts forever / Heritage to Israel / His Mercy lasts forever / He noticed our low estate //

His Mercy lasts forever / Saved us from our enemies / His Mercy lasts forever / He gives food unto all flesh //

His Mercy lasts forever / Oh, give thanks to Heaven's God / His Mercy lasts forever

CHAPTER 137

"*Remembering Zion*"

By Babylon's rivers / We sat down and we wept / Remembering Zion / Our harps upon willows //

By the riverbanks there / Our captors made us sing / A song of joy and mirth / Sing a song of Zion //

A song within this dearth / How shall we sing this song / Within a heathen land / If I forget to pray //

Toward Jerusalem / Let my tongue cleave unto / The top part of my mouth / Jerusalem must be //

Above all joy to me / Lord, remember Eden / In Jerusalem's pain / Who said to burn her down //

To burn her to the ground / Daughter of Babylon / Who is to be destroyed / The man who destroys her //

As she has treated us / Who brings her judgment down / Shall be a happy man / Who takes your little ones //

To die amongst her stones

CHAPTER 138
"The Lord Will Perfect Me"

I will praise You, Oh Lord / Praise You wholeheartedly / Before all the false gods / Will I sing praise to You //
Toward Your Holy Place / Will I worship and praise / Praise Your Name for Your Truth / And Your Lovingkindness //
For You have lifted up / Your Word above Your Name / All kings will praise You, Lord / Your Words of righteous fame //
They will sing to the Lord / The glory of the Lord / Even though You are high / You hear the poor man's cry //
The proud You walk on by / Though I am in trouble / I know You will save me / You will stretch out Your Hand //
Against my enemies / And their wrath shall not stand / You save with Your Right Hand / And Your Hand shall save me //
The Lord will perfect me / And that which concerns me / Your Mercy, Oh Lord God / Endureth for ever //
Forsake me not, Oh Lord / I am Your Handiwork

CHAPTER 139
"How Precious Are Your Thoughts"

Oh Lord, You have searched me / Oh Lord, You have known me / You know when I sit down / You know when I rise up //
You know my deepest thoughts / You know all of my ways / You know each word I say / You know me front and back //
You placed Your Hand on me / This is too high for me / Too wonderful to see / I cannot venture there //
It is too much to seek / Where can I flee from You / Your Presence everywhere / Your Spirit is present //
No matter where I go / If I go to Heaven / You are already there / If I descend to Hell //
Behold, You are still there / If I take morning flight / Dwell in the deep blue sea / Your Hand shall lead me there //
Your Right Hand shall hold me / If I hide in darkness / Dark is as light to You / You have possessed my reins //

From in my mother's womb / I will praise You, Oh Lord / I am awesomely made / With wonder and with fear //

Marvelous Your Works here / Too marvelous to tell / And that I know right well / My strength was known to You //

When I in secret lay / Within my mother's womb / And in my lowest place / You saw me from the first //

Imperfect and unformed / In all continuance / Though I was yet unborn / How precious are Your Thoughts //

To me, Oh Mighty Lord / The greatness of them all / More than the sands and stars / And when awakes the dawn //

Your Spirit is not far / But I commune with You / Oh Great and Mighty Lord / Lord slay the wicked ones //

And violence departs / Your Name in vain they take / Speak evil in their hearts / I hate them that hate You //

With understanding know / They hate both me and You / Search me, Lord, know my heart / Try me, Lord, know my thoughts //

Uncover wicked ways / And thoughts that become things / And lead me in the way / To life everlasting

CHAPTER 140
"The Strength of My Salvation"

Deliver me from evil men / Oh Lord keep me from violence / From men who imagine mischief / And keep their minds focused on war //

Their tongue is sharp as a serpent / Adder's poisonous violence / Stop and think what the Lord can do / He is able to see you through //

Keep me from the hands of the wicked / Oh Lord, from the violent man / They have tried to overthrow me / This is their purpose and their plan //

The proud have hid a trap for me / And cords to trip me where I walk / A wayside net they set for me / They have laid many snares for me //

Stop and think what the Lord can do / He is able to see You through / I said unto God Almighty / You are my God, Oh Lord, please hear //

The voice of my supplication / Oh God the Lord, mighty in battle / God the strength of my salvation / You covered my head in battle //

Oh Lord, come against evil plans / Undo the wicked man's device / Lest they exalt themselves in pride / Stop and think what the Lord can do //

He is able to see you through / As for the evil commanders / Of those who compass me about / Let their own mischief cover them //

Let their evil plans be found out / Let coals of fire fall upon them / Let them fall in their fiery trap / Into the pits which they have dug //

Let them fall, not to rise again / Let the violent man be chased / Until he be all overthrown / I know that the Lord will maintain //

The cause of the afflicted man / Defend the right of the poor man / The righteous will give thanks to God / Unto Your Name will he give praise //

The upright shall be in Your Word / In Your Presence their voice is heard

CHAPTER 141
"My Eyes Are on You, Oh God"

Lord, I cry Unto You / Lord, make haste to hear me / Give ear unto my voice / When I cry out to Thee //

Make my prayer as incense / The lifting of my hands / As evening sacrifice / Given by Your Command //

Set a watch over me / My mouth, my life, my tongue / Keep my heart from evil things / Wicked works, evil men //

And iniquity / Keep me from their poison / Let the righteous strike me / It shall be a kind deed //

And let him reprove me / For an excellent oil / Which shall not break my head / And I shall pray for them //

In their times of great need / When their fortunes reverse / In dangerous places / My words shall comfort them //

As sweetness to their souls / Even though our bones be / Scattered at the grave's mouth / Like the extra cleaving //

From cut wood on the Earth / My eyes are on You, Lord / Oh God, You will be there / My trust is in You, Lord //

Do not make my soul bare / Keep my soul from the snares / Which they have laid for me / Traps which they have set //

Who work iniquity / Let the evil workers / Fall into their own nets / Show me how to escape //

And live in Your Presence

CHAPTER 142
"My Refuge and My Portion"

I cried unto the Lord with my voice / Made my supplication with my voice / I poured out my soul's complaint to Him / I showed Him the trouble I was in //

My spirit was overwhelmed within me / Then You knew the path set before me / In the way in which I walked daily / They secretly laid a trap for me //

I looked on my right hand and I searched / But there was no man that would help me / None sought after me or cared for me / I cried to You, Lord, and said, You are //

My Refuge and my Portion on earth / Help me, for I am brought very low / My foes follow wherever I go / They are stronger than I can fight back //

Deliver me from prisoner's chains / So that I may praise Your Holy Name / Righteous souls shall compass me about / Bountifully You shall bring me out

CHAPTER 143
"Your Lovingkindness in the Morning"

Her my prayer, Oh Lord, give ear to me / In Your Faithful Righteousness hear me / Answer my requests in Your Mercy / And enter not to judgment with me //

No man is justified in Your Sight / The enemy has come for my soul / He has smitten me down to the ground / He has forced me to live in darkness //

As those that are planted underground / My spirit is overwhelmed in me / My heart is desolate within me / I remember how it used to be //

I meditate on Your Mighty Works / I think about the Works of Your Hands / I stretch out my hands unto You, Lord / I thirst after You, as in a drought //

Meditate on all the Lord can do / All the things the Lord has done for you / Hear me quickly Lord, I am falling / Hide not, lest I descend to the pit //

Please show Your Mercy so I may hear / Your lovingkindness in the morning / I trust You, Lord, show me how to walk / I lift up my soul to You, my God //

Deliver me from my enemies / I know that You are my hiding place / Teach me Your will, for You are my God / Lead me to the land of the righteous //

Quicken me for Your Name's sake, Oh Lord / Bring me out for Your Righteousness' sake / Cut off my foes for Your Mercy's sake / Destroy all them that afflict my soul //

For I am Your Servant, Oh Lord

CHAPTER 144
"That People Whose God is the Lord"

Blessed be the Lord my Strength / He teaches my hands to war / Teaches my fingers to fight / He is my Goodness //

He is my Fortress / He is my Defense / He is my Deliverer / My Shield and my Trusted Friend //

He helps me lead my people / Lord, what are mere men / That you notice them / Or the sons of men //

That You take account of them / Man is vain in his pursuits / A passing shadow is he / Come from Heaven, Lord //

Touch the mountains, Lord / And mountains will smoke / Cast lightning, and scatter them / Shoot arrows, and destroy them //

Send Your Power from above / Save me from drowning / From stranger's children / Full of vanity //

Given over to lying / I will sing a new song, Lord / The psaltery and the harp / Will bring praise to You //
You give victory / To kings in battle / To save David Your Servant / From the sword of all his foes //
Deliver me from strangers / Full of vanity / Given to lying / Let our sons be strong //
As young plants grown up in strength / And our daughters corner stones / Polished, royal, beautiful / Keep our barns quite full //
Of many good crops / To feed our sheep well / That they may bring forth / Thousands and thousands of sheep //
That our oxen may be strong / In labor, also / Happy in their stalls / Keep us safe at home //
City walls safe from attack / Citizens safe in their homes / Happy are such a people / Known as the people //
God knows, that people / Whose God is the Lord

CHAPTER 145
"The Virtues of My God"

I will extol the virtues of my God / And bless Your Name forever and ever / You are the Royal God, my King / You are the Praiseworthy God //
I will praise and bless Your Name / Forever and ever / You are the Great God, greatly to be praised / You are the Infinite God //
With unsearchable greatness / You are the Generational God / All generations praise Your Works / And declare Your Actions //
You are the Majestic God / Filled with glorious honor / And wonderful works / You are the Active God //
Your actions are mighty and awesome / I will declare Your Greatness / You are the Good God / The memory of Your Goodness is great to all //
You are the Righteous God / I will sing of Your Righteousness / You are the Gracious God / You are the Compassionate God //
You are the Patient God / You are the Merciful God / You are the Universal God / Good to all and Merciful over all //
You are the God of All Saints / All Your Works praise You / All Your Saints bless You / You are the God of All Power //

Your Saints tell of Your Mighty Actions / And Your Glorious, Majestic Kingdom / You are the God Of All Dominion / Your Kingdom is everlasting //

Your Dominion is enduring / You are the God Of All Support / You pick up all who fall / You raise up all who are bowed down //

You are the God Of All Provision / All eyes are on You / You give meat when it is due / You are the God Of All Desire //

You open Your Hand / You satisfy every desire / You are the Holy God / Righteous in all Your ways //

Holy in all Your Works / You are the Near God / Close to all who call on You / Who call on You in truth //

You are the True God / You are the Filling God / Fulfilling the desire / Of them that revere Your Awesomeness //

You are the Awesome God / You are the Hearing God / You will hear the cry of them that call You / You are the Saving God //

You will save them when they cry out to You / You are the Preserving God / You preserve all them that love You / You are the Judging God //

You pronounce judgment / Of destruction to all the wicked / You are the Eternal God / My mouth shall praise You //

You are the God Of The Holy Name / Let all flesh bless Your Holy Name / Forever and ever

CHAPTER 146
"Praise the Lord, Oh My Soul"

Praise the Lord, praise the Lord Oh my soul / I live to praise the Lord / I live to sing His Praises / Trust not in princes //

Trust not in man / His fleeting breath fails, and he dies / His thoughts perish with him / Trust in God, the God of Jacob //

He will help those whose trust is in Him / Who made sky and land and sea / And all life within all three / Who keeps truth forever //

Who gives justice to the oppressed / Who gives food to the hungry / The Lord sets the captives free / The Lord makes the blind eyes see //

The Lord lifts the oppressed ones / The Lord loves the righteous ones / The Lord preserves the strangers / The Lord relieves the orphans //

The Lord protects the widows / The Lord requites the wicked / The Lord reigns forevermore / Praise the Lord, Oh Zion //

Praise the Lord, all nations / Praise the Lord, all generations / Praise the Lord, praise the Lord Oh my soul

CHAPTER 147
"Praise the Lord, Oh Jerusalem"

Praise the Lord, for it is good / To sing praises unto our God / Praise the Lord, for it is pleasing / To sing praises unto our God //

Praise the Lord, for it is beautiful / To sing praises unto our God / The Lord is building Jerusalem / The Lord is gathering His People //

From around the world / The Lord is healing the brokenhearted / The Lord is binding up the wounded / The Lord knows all the stars by their names //

The Lord is great, and His Power great / The Lord has infinite understanding / The Lord lifts up the meek / The Lord casts down the wicked //

Sing a song unto the Lord / With thanksgiving sing unto God / Sing a song unto the Lord / With thanksgiving sing unto God //

Sing a song unto the Lord / With praise on the harp play unto God / Who blankets the heavens with clouds / Who causes the rain to fall down //

Who makes grass grow on mountain peaks / The Lord feeds the wild animals / The Lord feeds the ravens that cry / The Lord delights not in the horse's strength //

The Lord delights not in the runner's speed / The Lord delights in them that fear Him / The Lord delights in them that hope in Him / Praise the Lord, Oh Jerusalem //

Praise Your God, Oh Zion / The Lord strengthens the bars of your gates / The Lord blesses your children that play / The Lord makes your borders to be safe //

The Lord fills you with food that is great / The Lord sends His Commands through the earth / The Lord sends swift answers through

His Word / The Lord blankets winter with the snow // The Lord scatters crystals of the ice / The Lord sends the bitter winter winds / The Lord calls the spring winds to blow in / He causes winds to blow and waters flow //

That melt the ice and deep-encrusted snow / He opens His Word unto Jacob / His Laws and Judgments to Israel / This He did for no other nation //

Other nations know not His Judgments / Praise ye the Lord

CHAPTER 148
"The Praise of His Faithful Ones"

Praise ye the Lord from the Heavens / Praise ye the Lord from the High Places / Praise ye the Lord, all His Angels / Praise ye the Lord, all His Armies //

Praise ye the Lord, Sun and Moon / Praise ye the Lord, shining stars / Praise ye the Lord, heavens of heavens / And the waters above the heavens //

Praise the Name of the Lord, / For at His Word they were created / The Lord established them forever / The Lord made an eternal decree //

Praise the Lord in all the Earth / Sea creatures and the deepest oceans / Fire and hail, snow and mist / Stormy gales that blow at His Command //

Mountains and hillsides, fruit trees and cedars / Wild beasts and cattle, creeping things and birds / Kings and their subjects, princes and judges / Young men and women, old men and children //

Praise the Name of the Lord, all ye people / For the Name of the Lord is exalted / His Glory is above all earth and sky / He lifts up the strength of His People //

He lifts up the praise of His Faithful Ones / A people dear unto His Heart / Praise ye the Lord

CHAPTER 149
"Praise Him with a New Song"

Praise ye the Lord / Praise Him with a new song / In the congregation //
Let Israel rejoice / In the Lord who made him / Let Zion's children joy //
In praises to their King / Let them praise Him in dance / Let them praise Him in song //
Let them praise Him with harp / Praise him with tambourine / For the Lord delights in His People //
He shows the humble His Salvation / Let the saints rejoice in God's Glory / Let them sing for joy upon their beds //
Let them sing the High Praises of God / Let them hold a Two-Edged Sword in their hands / To exact God's Judgment on the heathen //
And His Punishments on the people / To bind their kings with chains of affliction / And their nobles with iron shackles //
To exact God's Judgment written for them / This honor is reserved for His Saints / Praise ye the Lord

CHAPTER 150
"Praise Ye the Lord"

Praise ye the Lord / Praise God in the Sanctuary //
Praise Him in the Highest Heaven / Praise Him for His Actions of Great Power //
Praise Him for His Excellence in Greatness / Praise Him with the Shofar of the Lord //
Praise Him with the psaltery and harp / Praise Him with the tambourine and dance //
Praise Him with stringed instruments and flutes / Praise Him upon the clanging cymbals //
Praise Him upon the crashing cymbals / Let everything that breathes praise the Lord //
Praise ye the Lord

Index

CHAPTER 1: "BLESSED IS THE MAN"
CHAPTER 2: "I HAVE SET MY KING"
CHAPTER 3: "MY PROTECTING SHIELD"
CHAPTER 4: "STAND IN AWE"
CHAPTER 5: "BE MY LEADER, OH MY LORD"
CHAPTER 6: "MY TEARS ARE MY OFFERING"
CHAPTER 7: "LET WICKEDNESS BE NO MORE"
CHAPTER 8: "LORD, YOU ARE OUR LORD"
CHAPTER 9: "GOD IS A REFUGE"
CHAPTER 10: "THE LORD IS THE KING"
CHAPTER 11: "HIS HOLY THRONE"
CHAPTER 12: "THE FINEST THINGS"
CHAPTER 13: "HEAR ME NOW"
CHAPTER 14: "GOD NEVER FAILS"
CHAPTER 15: "HE WHO WALKS WITH UPRIGHTNESS"
CHAPTER 16: "YOU ARE MY PORTION"
CHAPTER 17: "I WILL SURELY FOLLOW YOU"
CHAPTER 18: "THE SOURCE OF MY STRENGTH"
CHAPTER 19: "UPRIGHT CONFESSION"
CHAPTER 20: "THE LORD HEARS"
CHAPTER 21: "EXALT YOURSELF"
CHAPTER 22: "SAVE ME FROM THE LION'S ROAR"
CHAPTER 23: "THE LORD IS MY SHEPHERD"
CHAPTER 24: "THAT GLORIOUS KING"
CHAPTER 25: "KEEPER OF MY SOUL"
CHAPTER 26: "I LOVE TO LINGER IN YOUR HOLY HOUSE"
CHAPTER 27: "THE MOST IMPORTANT THING"
CHAPTER 28: "HE HEARD ME WHEN I CRIED"
CHAPTER 29: "GOD'S THUNDEROUS VOICE"
CHAPTER 30: "JOY COMES WITH THE MORNING LIGHT"
CHAPTER 31: "MY SPIRIT BELONGS TO YOU"
CHAPTER 32: "SURROUNDED BY MERCY"
CHAPTER 33: "HIS MERCIFUL MAJESTY"

CHAPTER 34: "I WILL BLESS THE LORD AT ALL TIMES"
CHAPTER 35: "PLEAD MY CASE, DEAR LORD"
CHAPTER 36: "YOUR UNFAILING LOVE"
CHAPTER 37: "THE INHERITANCE OF THE MEEK"
CHAPTER 38: "MY HOPE IS IN YOU"
CHAPTER 39: "WHAT TIME I HAVE HERE"
CHAPTER 40: "YOUR WILL, MY GOD, IS MY DELIGHT"
CHAPTER 41: "BE MERCIFUL UNTO ME, O LORD"
CHAPTER 42: "THE DEPRESSED, DISHEARTENED SOUL"
CHAPTER 43: "YOUR LIGHT AND YOUR TRUTH"
CHAPTER 44: "WE HAVE HEARD ABOUT YOU"
CHAPTER 45: "THE KING'S DAUGHTER"
CHAPTER 46: "WHEN COMES THE MORNING"
CHAPTER 47: "SING PRAISES"
CHAPTER 48: "TAKE A WALK ABOUT ZION"
CHAPTER 49: "SPEAKING OF WISDOM"
CHAPTER 50: "A DOUBLE ORDER"
CHAPTER 51: "CREATE A CLEAN HEART IN ME"
CHAPTER 52: "HE WHO TRUSTS IN HIS OWN STRENGTH"
CHAPTER 53: "THEY NEVER CALLED ON GOD"
CHAPTER 54: "GOD IS THE SOURCE OF MY HELP"
CHAPTER 55: "THE PRAYER OF THE BETRAYED"
CHAPTER 56: "I HAVE PLACED MY TRUST IN THE LORD"
CHAPTER 57: "A FIXED HEART ON YOUR GLORY"
CHAPTER 58: "STRANGERS TO RIGHTEOUSNESS"
CHAPTER 59: "BE MY DEFENSE"
CHAPTER 60: "PLEASE TURN TO US AGAIN"
CHAPTER 61: "LEAD ME TO THE ROCK"
CHAPTER 62: "THE EXCELLENCY OF MY EXPECTATION"
CHAPTER 63: "I WILL SEEK YOU EARLY"
CHAPTER 64: "JUST ONE OF HIS ARROWS"
CHAPTER 65: "SUNRISE SERVICE AND SUNSET PRAISES"
CHAPTER 66: "THE JOYFUL SOUND OF PRAISE"
CHAPTER 67: "LET ALL THE PEOPLE PRAISE YOU"
CHAPTER 68: "THE GOD OF OUR SALVATION"
CHAPTER 69: "THE TRUTH OF YOUR SALVATION"
CHAPTER 70: "MY HELP AND MY DELIVERER"

CHAPTER 71: "THE STRENGTH OF GOD ALMIGHTY"

CHAPTER 72: "LET THE WHOLE EARTH BE FILLED WITH HIS GLORY"

CHAPTER 73: "INTO THE SANCTUARY"

CHAPTER 74: "WHY HAVE YOU CAST US OFF?"

CHAPTER 75: "PROMOTION COMES FROM GOD"

CHAPTER 76: "WHEN GOD AROSE"

CHAPTER 77: "MY SONG IN THE NIGHT"

CHAPTER 78: "A TABLE IN THE WILDERNESS"

CHAPTER 79: "FOR THE GLORY OF YOUR NAME"

CHAPTER 80: "VISIT THIS VINE"

CHAPTER 81: "GOD OUR STRENGTH"

CHAPTER 82: "GOD STANDS IN THE CONGREGATION"

CHAPTER 83: "LET THEM KNOW YOU ARE LORD OF ALL"

CHAPTER 84: "EVEN THE SPARROW HAS FOUND HER PLACE"

CHAPTER 85: "I WILL HEAR WHAT THE LORD HAS TO SAY"

CHAPTER 86: "WHOLEHEARTED PRAISE"

CHAPTER 87: "THE LORD'S COUNTDOWN"

CHAPTER 88: "I HAVE STRETCHED OUT MY HANDS TO YOU"

CHAPTER 89: "YOUR MERCY COVENANT"

CHAPTER 90: "OUR DWELLING PLACE"

CHAPTER 91: "IN THE SECRET PLACE"

CHAPTER 92: "IT IS A GOOD THING"

CHAPTER 93: "THE LORD REIGNS"

CHAPTER 94: "SHOW YOURSELF, GOD"

CHAPTER 95: "COME LET US SING"

CHAPTER 96: "SING UNTO THE LORD A NEW SONG"

CHAPTER 97: "ZION HEARD ALL ABOUT IT"

CHAPTER 98: "ALL THE EARTH HAS SEEN HIS SALVATION"

CHAPTER 99: "EXALT THE LORD GOD ON HIGH"

CHAPTER 100: "MAKE A JOYFUL NOISE"

CHAPTER 101: "I WILL WATCH THE FAITHFUL ONES"

CHAPTER 102: "HE HEARS THE PRISONER'S CRY"

CHAPTER 103: "BLESS THE LORD, OH MY SOUL"

CHAPTER 104: "HE WALKS ON THE WINGS OF THE WIND"

CHAPTER 105: "GIVE THANKS"

CHAPTER 106: "HIS MERCY IS FOREVER"

CHAPTER 107: "OH, THAT MEN WOULD PRAISE THE LORD"

CHAPTER 108: "BE EXALTED, OH, LORD"

CHAPTER 109: "THE STRENGTH OF THE POOR"

CHAPTER 110: "THE ROD OF YOUR STRENGTH"

CHAPTER 111: "I AM IN PRAISE WHOLEHEARTED"

CHAPTER 112: "THE GENERATION OF THE RIGHTEOUS"

CHAPTER 113: "HIS GLORY IS ABOVE ALL"

CHAPTER 114: "TREMBLING AT THE PRESENCE OF THE LORD"

CHAPTER 115: "TRUST IN THE LORD"

CHAPTER 116: "WHAT CAN I GIVE BACK TO THE LORD?"

CHAPTER 117: "GOD'S ETERNAL LOVE AND TRUTH"

CHAPTER 118: "HIS MERCY ENDURES FOREVER"

CHAPTER 119: "CHAPTER 119, OVERVIEW"

CHAPTER 119: "A HEART NOT DIVIDED" (ALEF)

CHAPTER 119: "A WORD NOT FORGOTTEN" (BET)

CHAPTER 119: "A LAW NOT FORSAKEN" (GIMEL)

CHAPTER 119: "A SOUL NOT EMBITTERED" (DALET)

CHAPTER 119: "A MIND NOT CORRUPTED" (HEH)

CHAPTER 119: "A TRUST NOT UNFOUNDED" (VAV)

CHAPTER 119: "A HOPE NOT DIVIDED" (ZAYIN)

CHAPTER 119: "A WAY NOT ABANDONED" (HET)

CHAPTER 119: "A LIFE NOT UNCHANGING" (TET)

CHAPTER 119: "A HAND NOT UNFAITHFUL" (YUD)

CHAPTER 119: "A LOVE NOT UNCARING" (KAF)

CHAPTER 119: "A FAITH NOT RETIRING" (LAMED)

CHAPTER 119: "A TASTE NOT OVERLOOKED" (MEM)

CHAPTER 119: "A PATH NOT UNLIGHTED" (NUN)

CHAPTER 119: "A SHIELD NOT UNPOLISHED" (SAMEKH)

CHAPTER 119: "A RULE NOT DEVALUED" (AYIN)

CHAPTER 119: "A STEP NOT UNORDERED" (PEH)

CHAPTER 119: "A ZEAL NOT ABATED" (TZADEH)

CHAPTER 119: "A VOICE NOT WAVERING" (KUF)

CHAPTER 119: "A TRUTH NOT STOPPABLE" (RESH)

CHAPTER 119: "A STAND NOT CHANGEABLE" (SHIN)

CHAPTER 119: "A SOUL NOT SEPARATE" (TAV)

CHAPTER 120: "DELIVERANCE FROM DECEIT"

CHAPTER 121: "SOUL PRESERVER"

CHAPTER 122: "I WAS GLAD"

CHAPTER 123: "OUR EYES WAIT ON THE LORD OUR GOD"

CHAPTER 124: "IF GOD HAD NOT BEEN ON OUR SIDE"

CHAPTER 125: "THE LORD SURROUNDS HIS PEOPLE"

CHAPTER 126: "THEY THAT SOW IN TEARS"

CHAPTER 127: "UNLESS THE LORD BUILD THE HOUSE"

CHAPTER 128: "HE THAT FEARS THE LORD"

CHAPTER 129: "THEY WHO FOUGHT ME DID NOT WIN"

CHAPTER 130: "OUT OF THE DEPTHS"

CHAPTER 131: "LET ISRAEL HOPE IN THE LORD"

CHAPTER 132: "LORD, REMEMBER DAVID"

CHAPTER 133: "THE OINTMENT OF UNITY"

CHAPTER 134: "BLESS YE THE LORD"

CHAPTER 135: "PRAISE YE THE LORD"

CHAPTER 136: "HIS MERCY LASTS FOREVER"

CHAPTER 137: "REMEMBERING ZION"

CHAPTER 138: "THE LORD WILL PERFECT ME"

CHAPTER 139: "HOW PRECIOUS ARE YOUR THOUGHTS"

CHAPTER 140: "THE STRENGTH OF MY SALVATION"

CHAPTER 141: "MY EYES ARE ON YOU, OH GOD"

CHAPTER 142: "MY REFUGE AND MY PORTION"

CHAPTER 143: "YOUR LOVINGKINDNESS IN THE MORNING"

CHAPTER 144: "THAT PEOPLE WHOSE GOD IS THE LORD"

CHAPTER 145: "THE VIRTUES OF MY GOD"

CHAPTER 146: "PRAISE THE LORD, OH MY SOUL"

CHAPTER 147: "PRAISE THE LORD, OH JERUSALEM"

CHAPTER 148: "THE PRAISE OF HIS FAITHFUL ONES"

CHAPTER 149: "PRAISE HIM WITH A NEW SONG"

CHAPTER 150: "PRAISE YE THE LORD"

About the Author

Thomas D. "Denny" Hahn is currently the Music Director of First Pentecostal Church of New Orleans, Louisiana, and a Consulting Musician at Iglesia Pentecostal La Viña.

Denny has the soul of a poet. One year, he wrote 60 unique poems for families in his church as Christmas gifts.

He wrote most of Psalms in a Poem while recuperating from a major automobile accident.

He says of the project, "I give total credit to my Lord and Savior, Jesus Christ. He would speak words to my spirit in the wee hours of the morning. I could hardly speak during the day, but what glorious words the Shepherd of my Soul would speak to me late at night. I can truly say that because the Lord is my Shepherd, I shall not want for any good thing."

He was born on April 3, 1958, to the proud couple, Gary Lee and Mary Craft Hahn. They were a musical family. His father played the piano and sang, as did his mother. Later, Denny's sister Judy was born and would prove to be a fine singer as well.

Denny was in concert band, marching band, jazz band, ROTC band and choir at Southwood High School in Shreveport, Louisiana, where he attended three years. He graduated from Byram High School in Byram, Mississippi in 1976 while taking freshman courses at Jackson College of Ministries.

Denny graduated from Jackson College of Ministries in Jackson, Mississippi in 1979 with a major in music and a minor in theology.

OUR WRITTEN LIVES, LLC
WWW.OURWRITTENLIVES.COM

Our Written Lives provides publishing services to authors in various educational, religious, and human service organizations. For information, visit www.OurWrittenLives.com.

www.ingramcontent.com/pod-product-compliance
Lightning Source LLC
Chambersburg PA
CBHW030332100526
44592CB00010B/670